Praise for Brandi Morin

"[This] powerful and necessary work is required reading for all readers seeking to better know the realities and buried truths of the Indigenous experience." — *Booklist* (starred review)

"Brandi Morin is one of the most important Indigenous journalists and warriors of our time. Her raw, honest, and beautifully written story of her experiences, trauma, reliance, and perseverance is a must-read for all." — Crystal Echo Hawk, founder and executive director, IllumiNative

"*Our Voice of Fire* is a searingly honest, thought-provoking, and ultimately empowering exploration of pain and the quest for justice. By sharing her stories with the world, Brandi Morin makes a beautiful proclamation that there can be a hopeful path through trauma without diminishing the significance of the trauma itself, both personal and intergenerational. These are stories that need to be told and stories that need to be read." — Dan Levy

"Brandi Morin is a remarkable writer and a true original, her unique and clarion voice ringing out in the crowded field of contemporary journalism. This memoir is indeed written in fire: it can warm and it can scorch. And it casts a circle of light in the darkness." — Naomi Klein, author of *This Changes Everything*

"An indispensable memoir from one of the most informative voices in contemporary journalism. Brandi Morin's life story is one of dedication and triumph in spite of the many traumas inflicted upon Indigenous women by the settler colonial state. Through it all, her truth and hope persevere. This book will influence and inspire communities everywhere." — Waubgeshig Rice, author of *Moon of the Crusted Snow*

"Brandi Morin is a writer at the height of her powers, fighting to reclaim Canadian history for those whose memory has been crushed under the weight of it. Equal parts devastating and beautiful, *Our Voice of Fire* is essential reading for anyone who wants to understand Canada in 2022." — Christopher Curtis, journalist and co-founder of *The Rover*

"Throughout her remarkable career as a journalist, Brandi Morin has told the often-ignored stories of others — particularly of Indigenous women and girls — with respect, dignity, and fearless authenticity. In this book, she does the same with her own." — Jacqueline O'Neill, Canada's Ambassador for Women, Peace, and Security

"Brandi Morin is a fighter, a survivor, a champion, and her weapon of choice is her words. Only God/Creator knows where her fight for justice will take her next, but the way I see it, this is just the beginning." — Jolene Banning, journalist and producer

OUR VOICE OF FIRE

A MEMOIR OF A WARRIOR RISING

BRANDI MORIN

ANANSI

Copyright © 2022 Brandi Morin
Published in Canada in 2022 and the USA in 2022 by House of Anansi Press Inc.
www.houseofanansi.com

House of Anansi Press is committed to protecting our natural environment. This book
is made of material from well-managed FSC®-certified forests, recycled materials, and
other controlled sources.

House of Anansi Press is a Global Certified Accessible™ (GCA by Benetech) publisher.
The ebook version of this book meets stringent accessibility standards and is available
to students and readers with print disabilities.

26 25 24 23 22   2 3 4 5 6

Library and Archives Canada Cataloguing in Publication
Title: Our voice of fire : a memoir of a warrior rising / Brandi Morin.
Names: Morin, Brandi, author.
Identifiers: Canadiana (print) 2022020487X | Canadiana (ebook) 20220207127 | ISBN
9781487010577 (softcover) | ISBN 9781487010584 (EPUB)
Subjects: LCSH: Morin, Brandi. | LCSH: Women journalists—Canada—Biography.
| LCSH: Journalists—Canada—Biography. | CSH: First Nations women—Canada—
Biography. | CSH: First Nations—Canada—Biography. | CSH: First Nations
women—Canada—Social conditions. | CSH: First Nations—Canada—Social condi-
tions. | LCGFT: Autobiographies.
Classification: LCC E99.C88 M67 2022 | DDC 305.48/897323071092—dc23

Cover design: Alysia Shewchuk
Cover artwork: Sharifah Marsden, "Her Solo"
Text design and typesetting: Lucia Kim

*House of Anansi Press respectfully acknowledges that the land on which we operate is the
Traditional Territory of many Nations, including the Anishinabeg, the Wendat, and the
Haudenosaunee. It is also the Treaty Lands of the Mississaugas of the Credit.*

With the participation of the Government of Canada
Avec la participation du gouvernement du Canada | Canadä

*We acknowledge for their financial support of our publishing program the Canada Council for the
Arts, the Ontario Arts Council, and the Government of Canada.*

Printed and bound in Canada

MIX
Paper from
responsible sources
FSC® C103567

To my Creator, Yeshua, for never leaving or forsaking me; to my parents for giving me life and love; to my children, Faith, Luke, Dani, Elaysia, and Judah in heaven—I adore you all; to my beloved Kohkum in heaven; and to all MMIWG, to their families and loved ones, and to the survivors.

I am Brandi Morin.

I'm a proud Cree/Iroquois/Frenchwoman from the lands of my ancestors in Treaty 6 Territories of the Michel First Nation.

But I did not always know this.

For many years I was disconnected from my heritage, my history, and my birthright.

For many years my power was hidden in smoke and shadow, my voice lost to the darkness.

Prologue

- TINA -

I STOOD IN THE driveway of my friend's place and shifted impatiently from foot to foot, blowing on my hands for warmth. Springtime in Winnipeg doesn't exactly qualify as balmy, and that chilly morning in 2019 was no exception. I checked my phone for the hundredth time. Where were they? I'd barely slept last night, tossing and turning on the mattress on the floor in my friend's spare room. Morning seemed to take forever to arrive as it always does when you're anticipating something.

Finally, a white car pulled up and I jumped in the back seat. Two men sat in the front and my heart instantly jumped into my throat, as it did every time I had to ride in a stranger's car. I swallowed the fear and said a prayer. *This is a job, we are a team, and everything will work out*, I told myself.

Besides, I wasn't a helpless child anymore. I was thirty-eight years old and working on a story with the *New York Times*! Here was arguably the most important media outlet in the world looking to give attention to our people. In all my years as a journalist our stories had barely made the headlines in Canada. This was a huge breakthrough. *Finally, our voices will be heard, and maybe the world will start to care about the injustices happening here*, I thought to myself. I took a deep breath.

The man in the passenger seat turned around. He was about ten years older than me with short, nicely groomed facial stubble and tousled dark hair. He might have been able to pass for a shorter version of Clark Kent.

"Brandi," he said, his hand extended. "So nice to finally meet you. I'm Dan and this is Aaron Vincent, our photographer." He motioned towards the driver with his other hand. Heart racing, I pushed myself forward and shook his hand.

I knew who he was of course. Dan Bilefsky, Oxford University graduate and renowned journalist, who'd spent his early career travelling the world as a correspondent for the *Wall Street Journal* and the *Financial Times* before returning home to Montreal to work as Canadian correspondent exclusively for the NYT.

"This is my first time in Winnipeg, actually." His voice had an unfamiliar lilt to it.

"Okay, I'm curious. Where is your accent from?" I asked.

He chuckled. "Yeah, I get that a lot. You see, I've lived all over the world and speak a few languages, so French is the dominant accent, but there's a mix of London English, and an influence from my time spent in Brussels."

"Pretty neat," I said with a gulp. Like he wasn't intimidating enough. *But,* I reminded myself, *I am the one who reached out to him and he is the one who said yes.*

A FEW MONTHS BEFORE, I had emailed him on a whim to ask him whether the NYT was interested in commissioning Indigenous stories. If so, I was the person they were looking for. To my surprise, Dan answered and said they were *hungry* for Indigenous content. (Yes, he used the word *hungry!*)

Then, a couple of weeks ago, Dan emailed me. "I finally have an Indigenous story to do ASAP and I would love to work with you on it," he wrote. My pulse skipped. *OMG, Brandi, just keep your cool.*

He continued, "The story is this: the government,

as you probably know, will soon be coming out with its long overdue report on disappeared and murdered Indigenous women and girls. I would like to write a story ahead of the report that would ideally focus on one very compelling survival narrative and talk to families of people who lost their daughters."

I was familiar with the issue. It was something I'd been writing about for years as an Indigenous reporter. The vanishing and murder of our women has been ongoing since 1492, but governments and police agencies only began reluctantly documenting this crisis over the last few decades. And their motivation to respond has been practically non-existent. This, despite the fact that all across North America, Indigenous women and girls are disproportionately targeted by violence. A few years ago, the cries for justice from the families and survivors started to be heard in the mainstream. This had compelled the National Inquiry into Missing and Murdered Indigenous Women and Girls (MMIWG). The report Dan was referring to was the long overdue finding from the commissioners, scheduled for release in June 2019.

I had no idea if the report's recommendations would make any difference whatsoever, but here was the NYT wanting to cover it! Too often in this business, especially as an Indigenous person, we need to fight for our stories to reach the mainstream. It's a continual push to convince editors that our stories are worthy of the spotlight. And when the rare story does hit the global circuit, there's a long history of non-Indigenous reporters getting it wrong — resulting in a legacy of mistrust between the media and Indigenous communities. I was determined to do everything in my power to make sure the media got *this* story right. I emailed Dan back and asked how I could help.

He asked me to be his "fixer." To be honest, I didn't even know what that was. He said he wanted to connect with some of the families and wondered if I knew anyone who would be a good subject to feature. The word *subject* didn't sit well with me. We — they — are people and these are incredibly painful stories to recall. But yes, I had several ideas of who to approach so I answered yes and then googled the term *fixer*.

My heart sank as I read that a fixer is someone who helps journalists in a foreign nation navigate the culture and countryside. I was a reporter. I wanted to help write this story, not just provide an "in" with Indigenous families. So I pushed back, and to my delight, Dan said that it might be possible for me to co-write the piece and get my name in the NYT as a contributor. Well, all I needed was a foot in the door in order to kick it down.

We decided to focus the story on the murder of Tina Fontaine, a fifteen-year-old First Nations girl whose tiny body had been wrapped in a duvet, weighed down with stones, and dumped in the Red River in Winnipeg, in the summer of 2014.

I'd watched the newsreels of a tow truck lifting her body covered by a tarp from the river. Those images had played over and over in my head for weeks. My guts churned for this child who was taken so easily and so callously. Fifty-three-year-old Raymond Cormier was arrested and charged with second-degree murder in her killing but was acquitted in 2018. Her murder is still unsolved.

Something about Tina's young, beautiful, innocent-looking face splattered across headlines shook the nation. Perhaps it was the fact that she looked like any other girl — other than her brown skin. Perhaps it was the way her body was disposed of like trash. Whatever it was about this child's murder, people finally saw our women and girls as human beings — not just another dead Indian, a runaway, or a hopeless drunk on a bender.

Tina's murder woke people up to the crisis. Her short, tragic life helped shift public opinion to support a

national inquiry — something that Indigenous communities had been demanding for years. So Tina's story was
the right one to revisit in connection to the report's final
findings all these years later, but I knew there was always
a cost to the family when reopening these wounds.

I called Thelma Favel, Tina's great-auntie and the
person who had raised her, to request an in-person
interview. She informed me that she was taking a break
from the media. She'd given countless interviews over
the years and had endured the prodding for the sake of
Tina, but each time it was draining and excruciatingly
painful for her. And so often, the way Tina's story was
retold broke her heart. But as we spoke, I felt her soften.
I knew my voice was comforting to her — the nuances
are familiar in Indian Country even if our nations and
cultures are deeply varied. I also sensed she understood
that I actually cared and I wasn't just some robotic
reporter looking to come in, take a piece of her life,
and push an insensitive story out. She decided that she
wanted to do it, "to give Tina a voice from the grave."
Her words choked me up and I shuddered at the sudden
vision I had of the thousands of women and girls whose
souls are roaming the lands of this nation, voiceless, yet
calling for justice.

I thought about all of this and more from the back

seat of the car as we drove two hours north to Thelma's house just outside of Sagkeeng First Nation. It was a chilly, windy day. The ground was brown with barren leftovers from a cold northern winter. Thelma's home looked like a typical small, one-storey rez house with chipped paint on the bottom half of the siding. The yard was tidy and quiet, the winter-brittle grass was long on one side of the house and surrounded a worn trampoline that seemed to release the echoes of children reaching toward the sky.

Tina once played there.

I prayed under my breath as I led the way up the wooden porch steps and knocked on the front door. The sharp wind stirred my hair and the hem of my long black cotton dress that peeked from underneath my coat.

"Hello?" a small voice answered from within. Thelma pulled open the door and my heart sank when I saw her. She was hunched and grey. Not just her hair, but her whole countenance seemed to seep a deep grey sorrow.

"*Tansi* (hello, how are you?). Thelma, it's good to meet you." I stepped inside and embraced her. I felt her energy flow into mine and mine back to her. A small flicker of hope sparked in her tired eyes.

Dan and Aaron stepped inside at my prompting. "Hello, Thelma, I'm sorry to meet you under such circumstances, but thank you for having us to your home," said Dan, greeting her with a two-handed handshake.

She invited us into her small living room and we all fell into the big, comfy, beige couches. As Dan began his interview, I took in my surroundings while keeping one ear on the conversation. Almost every square inch of the room's walls were filled with framed photos of family members. Many of them were of Tina at various stages of her life — from a little girl of five or six to one of her when she was ten, then one taken not long before she died. I was sitting in the space where she once laughed, played, got into trouble, cried, and hugged her auntie Thelma, whom she called Mom.

I overheard Thema telling Dan that they used to watch crime documentaries together in this room while Tina sat on the floor painting her toenails.

Something began to shift uncomfortably in my chest and I felt a dull heat in the pit of my stomach.

Thelma was filling Dan in on some of Tina's troubled past. I knew most of it already — she had been a lost little girl, passed through the rough hands of the provincial foster- and group-home systems for most of her life. But she was strong of spirit and she often defied authority and ran away whenever she could.

My palms were now sweating and I felt as if a bonfire were roaring in my belly. What was wrong with me?

And then I saw something that scared me. It was me on those walls. My small face as a child was staring out from all those photos. The same gaps in years exist in my childhood photo album because I too had been bouncing between foster care and my own home, doing my best to survive through defiance and running.

I closed my eyes. I needed to keep it together. I was a professional reporter. I had no business getting emotional. When I focused again on the photos, Tina was back in the frame. And that was where she would remain. She would never make more memories.

My mind flashed to the image of her body in the Red River. Another memory flared in my mind alongside it — a bloody condom floating in the toilet waiting to be flushed. Drums were banging in my head now: *Tina died. I survived. Tina died. I survived. I am her. She is me.*

I bit my lip until it almost bled and pinched my wrist to stop myself from breaking down in front of Dan, Aaron, and Thelma. *No, no, no.*

"I keep the curtains drawn all the time since Tina died," said Thelma. "I can't open them because when

I look out there and down the road...I can see Tina walking home. I see her coming back to me and then I realize...she's not there."

Tears filled her eyes, and she stopped. Dan handed her some Kleenex from a box on the coffee table and she wiped her tears, blew her nose, and continued gripping the dirty tissue for comfort afterwards. Everyone was silent. I couldn't hold it back anymore and I allowed my own tears to break free. They flowed down my face like a slow stream, bringing some relief to the internal heat consuming my body.

After about an hour-long interview, Dan handed it over to me and I asked Thelma what she hoped would come from the National Inquiry's findings.

"Well, it came too late, and honestly, I don't have faith in it—in them. The government or others didn't care then, so I don't trust them." Thelma's anger was more than justified. Tina had technically been in the custody of Child and Family Services when she'd been murdered. In the twenty-four hours before her disappearance she was seen by provincial child welfare workers, police officers, and health-care professionals. None of them helped her despite the fact that she was intoxicated and in the company of a strange man—Raymond Cormier. Even when she came to the hospital, a fifteen-year-old who was so under the influence of unknown substances that she was barely conscious, they didn't keep her. They didn't help her. They dumped her back on the streets. The next time she was seen, she was wrapped in a duvet in the river. Tina's nightmare hours before her death were the reason Thelma hoped to start a twenty-four-hour youth outreach centre in Tina's name in the hopes that no other young person seeking help would be turned away.

After we left Thelma's house, we drove to Tina's gravesite, which was less than ten minutes away. It took us a while to find her grave but when I saw it, imagining her little body buried under my feet made my knees shake. There were letters, plastic flowers, and ornaments left there in front of her heart-shaped marble grave marker. She was buried alongside her father, Eugene Fontaine, who was beaten to death in Winnipeg in 2011. I heard that Tina never got over the death of her dad — she was close to her father, as I am to mine. My feet felt like they were sinking into the ground, as if I were being pulled into the earth to join Tina in her grave. Again, I told myself to keep it together. I was on a job. But part of me knew this wasn't true.

I wasn't just a reporter. This wasn't just a job. This was my life too. This was my story.

It was *our* story.

. . .

SOME TWO WEEKS LATER the feature was published in the NYT and yes, I did get a contributor line. I was invigorated. I still dream of one day having my own byline in the *New York Times*, not as a contributor, but as a sole author. Because when my name gets there, so do all my relations — the Tina Fontaines, the aunties, mothers, sisters, cousins, daughters, and friends who have never had a voice in the world. And so, I press on.

- 1 -

I SLIPPED INTO THE private hospital room and took a deep breath. It was a grey, cold day in October 2008. Outside the window the wind was shaking the trees into a frenzy. Inside the room, it was perfectly still and quiet. My kohkum (grandmother) was lying in the bed beneath white sheets, her breathing was shallow and slow, and her once plump face was sunken. My mother and stepfather were in the room and Mom smiled and beckoned me to join her where she was perched at the head of the bed. I approached softly knowing that any noise amplified the constant pain my kohkum was in.

I was scared to even touch her, but I gently took Kohkum's hand and sat in silence feeling her finger bones and knuckles protruding through her papery skin. My heart ached to witness this once strong and quick-witted matriarch of the family so decimated by cancer. Here was the woman who had always been my anchor. She'd held me fast with her unconditional acceptance and love when I believed myself to be utterly unlovable. She'd been my safe harbour throughout my stormy and tumultuous childhood.

Suddenly I was that twelve-year-old again, running to my kohkum when my life was in danger, knowing that in her arms even the most ferocious monsters could not touch me. And then I was back in the hospital room once more, a twenty-eight-year-old woman. The tables were turned. She was weak and I was the strong one. It was surreal seeing my beloved kohkum so helpless, but at the same time I felt an awe and appreciation for having the chance to comfort her.

Mom said it was time to put her curlers in. I was a bit shocked that even in this state Kohkum wanted her hair done. Then again, Kohkum's appearance was always important to her. I always thought of her as the native Elizabeth Taylor. She embodied beauty and elegance with her dark, dramatically made-up eyes, striking cheekbones, and cropped hairdo dyed a luxurious shade of burgundy. Every night she slept in old-fashioned rollers so that she'd have her signature curly look the next day. Whether she was staying home, going on a shopping trip, out to bingo, or to a fancy occasion, Kohkum wanted to look good doing it.

Mom handed me the hairbrush and I began gently brushing what was left of Kohkum's withering hair, now the colour of watered-down wine with a line of grey creeping up from the roots. *She wouldn't be happy about these greys*, I thought. As I started slowly wrapping her hair around the first barrel of a pink curler, she yelped in pain. I froze. Mom motioned for me to keep going. This was what Kohkum said she wanted, and even though the slightest movement caused her immense discomfort, she was as determined as ever to have her way. And Mom and I were equally determined to fulfill her wish and get those curlers in. So I continued.

I had never seen someone close to me die. I'd lost my other grandmother, Mémère, but I hadn't been close with her. She'd never gotten over the fact that my dad had married an Indian girl and not a French one. Mémère didn't like the idea of Indians in the family and for much of my life I felt like she considered me an outsider. I know she loved us, it was just an arm's-length kind of love.

Kohkum, in contrast, was like my second mother. As I slowly wrapped wispy strand by wispy strand, my favourite memories of Kohkum flashed through my mind like a multi-sensory slide show.

I could almost smell and taste her chicken soup. Hot and soothing with carrots, tomatoes, noodles, and chicken spiced exactly right with garlic and something else. I didn't know what that other ingredient was and I regretted not getting the recipe from her, knowing that I wouldn't taste it again.

I saw her large wood-framed 1970s-style photo of Elvis in my mind's eye. It graced the wall of her living room for years. She adored the stunningly handsome, hip-shaking, flashy, spirit-moving singer and she passed down her love of the King of Rock 'n' Roll to me.

I thought of the homes and apartments she'd lived in over the years. I spent more time at Kohkum's than I did at my own home in my preteen and teen years. Kohkum just got me. Even though at the time I was a lost, mixed-up kid who resisted authority and seemed determined to get into trouble, she accepted me fully. When I was at Kohkum's I felt a steadiness I couldn't find anywhere else, and the fact that she let me smoke cigarettes with her put her in my cool books. We were tight. We shared her bed when I stayed with her and I loved her chaotic room. Clothes, perfume bottles, bingo dabbers, books, and gossip magazines were strewn everywhere. On her dresser lay piles of half-used makeup, more perfume, curlers, hair pins, and miscellaneous delights. She had a wooden jewellery chest with multiple drawers—more of a treasure chest overflowing with vintage costume jewellery and colourful statement pieces that offset her beauty.

I smiled as I thought of how as an adult, my bedroom was chaotic and I too had a collection of eccentric jewellery. Just another inheritance from my kohkum.

Eventually it came time to do the back of Kohkum's hair. My stepdad lifted her forward and held her in place while I wrapped the final curlers. All the while, Kohkum cried out. I cried a little too, but not too much, because I still wasn't able to fully process that this was the end for her. Not Kohkum. She was indestructible.

When we'd finished, we jacked the bed up so Kohkum could sit for a while. My mom reached for a lone can of Pilsner beer, cracked it open, and inserted a straw. She held it below my kohkum's chin and she slowly took a gratifying sip of her favourite beer. A smile emerged.

There she was. That was the Kohkum I knew and loved. I laughed inside remembering the vigour of her spirit. When Kohkum was happy, everyone was happy. Her laugh was infectious and uncontrolled. And when she laughed, it was with her whole body and soul— humour was medicine. She was so expressive and dramatic that you couldn't help but be drawn into the wild ride of life with her. And it *was* a wild ride. Even into her seventies, Kohkum could outdrink anyone. She was famous for being able to hold her own on a drinking bender and nurse a box of Pilsner sometimes for days on end. She was the life of the party and people came from far and wide to let loose with her. There was always music in the form of live guitars, spoons, or the country station on the radio. After the last poor soul had passed out on a kitchen chair, the floor, or the couch, Kohkum would still be up riding her Pilsner buzz for hours afterwards.

But it wasn't always easygoing when Kohkum was drinking. You didn't want to be on the wrong side of her attention, and her shift in demeanour could be fierce when she was drunk. Over the years, I bore witness to the violent fights that broke out between other party-goers and her, although they were nothing compared to the drunken scraps that her children witnessed when she was younger and possessed even more vigour.

My uncle told me of an instance when he saw my kohkum scrapping with Ross, her boyfriend at the time. Ross was leaving the house and she came flying out the porch door and tossed a beer bottle at his face. Uncle said Ross's eyeball came right out of its socket. He held it in place and walked to the hospital. Not long after, they were back together as if nothing had happened.

But Kohkum's sobriety looked a lot like a bender as well. She'd go long stretches of confessing her sins at the Catholic church several times a day. Her rosary was always in hand as she faithfully rubbed the beads along each decade, praying with a repentant heart.

We were often subject to sudden bursts of sermons warning us of the apocalyptic disasters that loomed in the near future. When the moon turned blood-red and the skies black for three days, Jesus was coming back for the Rapture and we'd better be ready and right with Him. During those phases, my kohkum dealt in doom and gloom and I lived in terror of the upcoming Judgement Day. But despite the fear, I knew that Kohkum was driven by her love for us. I'd watch her get so caught up in prayer for the well-being and the salvation of her children and grandchildren that she'd passionately cry out to God in tears. I admired her love for her family. Maybe we were a broken family, maybe we were a family of extremes, but Kohkum's fierce love glowed at the centre and she never stopped believing in better days ahead for all of us.

Sometimes I couldn't understand the source of her optimism. From the little I knew of Kohkum's life, she'd been dealt a hand stacked with hardship and heartache. I knew vaguely that her childhood had been difficult. When she was ten, she lost her beloved father, as well as her older sister, to tuberculosis, and life at home with her new stepfather was tough. She spoke reverently of attending a "convent school" as a child but no further details were forthcoming.

She became a nurse's aide in the early 1950s and managed to blend into the white world. But she was always proud to be an Indian. She was pretty, well-spoken, and strong-willed. She could also be tough and stand her ground when she needed to.

She married early and, at first, seemed to have married well. Pépère was a good, hard-working Frenchman. He married Kohkum when she was four months pregnant with another man's baby. My mom told how Pépère took baby Greg as his own the moment he was born. He let it be known that when Greg died, he wanted him buried in Pépère's grave so father and son could be together for eternity.

But Kohkum and Pépère's marriage quickly turned turbulent. Over the next eleven years, Kohkum gave birth to nine children as the relationship between her and Pépère grew ever worse. Again from my mother, I knew the story of how my grandfather returned home one day armed with a rumour that Kohkum had been running around, and determined to teach her a lesson. He took her outside the city limits and beat her senseless, knocking out several teeth and almost killing her in the process.

My mother had been just a little girl and she'd hidden in terror from my kohkum because she was unrecognizable with her hair pulled out in spots, her swollen face, and her skin all black and blue. My pépère taught her a lesson, I guess. Their marriage didn't last too long afterwards and he moved to the Northwest Territories.

Money was tight for Kohkum her entire life. She scrounged her pennies and worked hard to raise her children on her own. A lot of times she required government assistance but she always managed to save enough money to buy gifts for birthdays and Christmas—showing her love through a sweater bought at Zellers or a sparkling watch from Shoppers Drug Mart. I'd been the recipient of this same devotion as her grandchild. Sometimes she'd live off chicken bologna sandwiches and rationed milk for days on end until her next paycheque. Despite that, she always took care of her own.

Kohkum didn't stop when her own children were raised either. She opened up her home to fostering Indigenous kids. She took in my uncle Lloyd when he was three years old. His biological mother had died tragically, but Kohkum became his mom and she was all he knew. She eventually adopted him.

My cousins Crystal and Holly came to live with Kohkum when they were toddlers as well. She raised them for most of their childhoods before a couple from Vancouver Island adopted them. Kohkum was anguished to let them go. They were her kids but she didn't have the financial resources to keep them and the goal of the system was to have them adopted. When they left there were lots of tears. She vowed never to change her phone number so they could always find her.

For years there had been no contact, but when the girls became teens they reached out to the family. We were all relieved to learn that they'd had a good life on the island and hadn't undergone the horror story that many adopted Indigenous children have experienced. Kohkum was the most relieved of all. The bonds of family were reconnected and we were safe. This was all she ever truly cared about. Well, that, her hair, and a nice cold can of Pilsner.

Not long after I did her hair at the hospital, Kohkum died. I wasn't with her. I simply could not process the news. I went to the funeral home and my mom ushered me over to spend time with Kohkum's body. She was cold. She didn't look like herself but her hair looked good. I was proud to have been the last one to have helped with that.

Other than that small surge of gratitude, I felt numb to Kohkum's passing. I couldn't understand why. I'm a passionate woman, like my mother and Kohkum. The women in our family express ourselves flamboyantly, we love deeply.

My mom was a wreck. She hadn't been close with Kohkum. They'd struggled with this for as long as my mom could remember. Soon after giving birth to my mother, Kohkum became pregnant once more and gave birth to a full-term, stillborn baby boy named Richard. It devastated her. She fell into the grips of mourning and depression and neglected to show my mother, who was still a baby, the proper love and affection she needed. This fractured bond remained with them for the rest of their lives. Kohkum's passing left Mom in a terrible state and she mourned openly and honestly. Then there was me. I'd just lost one of the most important people in my life but my eyes remained dry and my heart frozen.

In the middle of the night, about three days after the funeral, it hit me. Kohkum wouldn't be there to see my children grow up. I couldn't call her when times got tough just to hear her say it would be all right. I would never again hear her telling me she loved me and would see me soon. She'd never be able to rescue me again. I wasn't ready for a world without Kohkum.

I began sobbing so hard that the bed began to shake. I curled up in the fetal position and succumbed to grief. I called my mom. She told me it would be all right. "Everything you're feeling is normal," she murmured down the phone line. "This is what it feels like to mourn someone you love so deeply." She sounded so much like Kohkum in that moment that I smiled.

FOR MONTHS AFTERWARDS, KOHKUM visited often in my dreams. Although it was the oddest thing—her visits never felt like dreams, they felt real. She would show up and we would sit down and talk like old times. Sometimes we were in my mom's garage, or at one of her old apartments, or literally in the white clouds of heaven.

The first few times I asked her if it was okay for her to be there. I wanted to make sure she'd cleared these visits with God. She shrugged off my concern and said of course she could be there with me. I sensed that even in the afterlife, my kohkum still got what she wanted.

Her visits became less frequent, but she still showed up whenever I was going through something difficult in order to give me advice or comfort. These days she visits maybe once a year. When she does, I relish the time for our spirits to connect in the dream world.

But this isn't to say that my relationship with my kohkum is relegated solely to the dream world. I'd been wrong when I thought that Kohkum's death meant her ongoing influence in my life was over. She had plenty more to teach me.

AFTER SHE DIED MY aunties went through her home to organize and distribute her belongings. They called all the grandchildren together to decide what they wanted. No one wanted her chest of costume jewellery except for me. I was a little offended on behalf of Kohkum, but also grateful. To me these pieces were priceless treasures that allowed me to keep and cherish her essence forever.

My aunties also found scribblings of hers as well as several journals. Once they pieced them together, they had a sizable collection of her writing that they shared with the family. I had no idea that Kohkum was also a writer. Actually, I had no idea how much of Kohkum's life I hadn't known about at all! I devoured her writing, hungry to know more about the woman I missed so much.

She wrote about how much she loved hunting musk-rat in the bush with Daddy and her sister and how she excelled at track and field but wasn't picked for the school team. She wondered whether it was because she was native. Kohkum's writings also opened my eyes to darker elements of her past that she'd kept tucked away. After her daddy passed, her home life became a chaotic environment coloured by addiction and violence. She wrote in her diaries about how she'd steal her mother and stepfather's liquor bottles and pour water in them to try to slow their drinking down. When things got rowdy at home, she'd call the police and swear that she'd never grow up to be like them. I also learned that the "convent" she attended as a child was a residential school. But I didn't yet understand the significance of this fact.

But I did know that something had been kindled inside of me when I read my kohkum's words. Each small scrap of paper, each page in her journal, fed the spark of curiosity within until it was a roaring fire of need. I needed to know more. About Kohkum. About me. About my people.

Without my even realizing it, my feet were set on a new path. Over the next few years, I began to hunt for the truth through any means I could, from research to collecting personal stories. I learned about the horrors of residential schools, created with the express goal of indoctrinating Indigenous children into white culture through shame, violence, neglect, and punishment for daring to exist in the first place. I thought about my kohkum in that place — taught that she'd be damned if she didn't renounce her Indian heritage, the fear of hell's torture in the afterlife burned so deeply into her psyche that she'd suffered that torture throughout this life as well. No wonder she didn't talk about it.

I also began to learn of the richness, the wonders, the beauty, and the intricate legacy of my Indigeneity. It wasn't about a bunch of broken, drunken, lost, brown-skin-coloured people who made bannock and played bingo every other night. We were much more — and our identities were being stifled in the name of colonial agendas that attempted to wipe us out.

This desire to learn more set me on my path to becoming a journalist. I started covering the stories of Indigenous Peoples in the courts and on their lands. I went to prisons and protests. I learned to retell the stories that were being told to me. I began to use Kohkum's gift of writing that was passed on to me. My work as a journalist unleashed a desire for justice in me — as strong as a wildfire — to help transform the narrative of Indigenous oppression. Sometimes I feel as if I'm making up for lost time, for the things Kohkum didn't get to do.

MY MOTHER TOLD ME that the day before Kohkum died, she called all her children into the room so she could pray a blessing over them. They gathered around her bed and suddenly Kohkum began speaking Cree — the language of her ancestors that she spoke in childhood but had long forgotten. The words poured out of her, musical and mysterious, bathing her children in their cadence. Her first language to invoke her final blessing. The room crackled with power.

When Mom told me what had happened, my first reaction was an overwhelming regret that I had not been in the room.

Now I know that I didn't have to be.

Kohkum's ancestral blessing has been guiding my feet since the moment it roared into the world calling us to wake from our slumber and remember who we are.

Her words, like her tenacity, have been passed on to her children, grandchildren, and great-grandchildren. We rise as part of the living, breathing, blazing saga of her tremendous mark on this world.

- 2 -

AS A CHILD, I was dazzled by my parents.

My dad was so handsome, with his jet-black hair and hazel eyes, chiselled jawline and persuasive smile. People always said he resembled the late actor Michael Landon.

One of my favourite memories of Dad is when he would tell me stories before bed. Tucked in under the covers I would hear the porch door creaking from the wind and coyotes howling in the distance. It was the lullaby to accompany whatever tale my father was conjuring with his deep voice turned low into an almost whisper. I would listen in rapt wonder as he recounted adventures from his childhood, relishing the intimacy of it all.

I also cherish my memories of Dad with his horses. He's always been a passionate horseman, he just has a way with them. He could always see potential in the unwanted stragglers and then bring it out in them. Even the wild, stubborn ones learned to trust him. He'd channel a steady know-how and inner calmness that would win them over every time.

Perhaps you could say he is a rescuer of sorts. We didn't have much money but that didn't stop him from bringing home strays, from dogs to cars. My mother, struggling to raise four children, was not impressed whenever he brought back some rare old beater he'd found a deal on (and it was often). One time he came home with a black Cadillac that looked like a hearse from the 1940s. We all piled in, including Mom, and went for a joy ride down the highway, revelling in the nostalgia of it all.

Where my father was handsome, my mother has always been breathtakingly beautiful. With chestnut-coloured long wavy hair set against her piercing dark oval eyes and defined high cheekbones that she got from Kohkum—beauty was one of the only things, I imagine, that was steady in her life.

As a little girl, I would watch her put on her makeup and dream of one day growing up to look like her. Mom always tells the story of when I was in grade one and showed up in class with her makeup caked on. I'm

OUR VOICE OF FIRE

talking bright-pink blush slathered on my cheeks, heavy blue eyeshadow, and fire-engine-red lipstick! After a few days my teacher called my mom to inquire about my dramatic new look. Mom had no idea that I'd been sneaking into her stash in the bathroom and the next day she confronted me in the act. I was mortified and I felt my little cheeks redden under the layers of pink blush.

"Oh Brandi." She crouched down and looked me in the eyes, trying to hide her smirk of amusement. "Little girls don't wear makeup."

As she gently wiped off my makeup, I studied her face. The soft blue eyeshadow, the black liner outlining her eyes, and red lipstick glowing on her lips. "When you're older you can wear makeup like Mommy, okay?"

I was disappointed but agreed. I couldn't wait for the day when I could wear makeup whenever I wanted!

Mom took after Kohkum when it came to being headstrong and determined. (And I took after Mom.) Mom doesn't let anyone push her around. She always kept the house in tip-top shape and expected us to do the same. I hated cleaning and taking orders from Mom, who was militant in her demands. To this day I dislike cleaning—but I do it because I'm a mom now too.

My kohkum loved her kids, but she had her own demons. For most of my mom's childhood she experienced living in a volatile home with an alcoholic mother. Most of the time Mom and her siblings didn't have food, so in summertime they'd raid the neighbourhood gardens or knock on doors asking for something to eat. My kohkum often took off for days or weeks on party benders, leaving the kids to fend for themselves. Or she'd bring the party home, exposing her children to the dangers of violent drunken fights and leaving them vulnerable to sexual abuse.

At twelve my mom quit school and moved out on her own. She met my dad when she was fifteen and they fell madly in love. By seventeen she had her first child, my older sister. And just like Kohkum's, my mother's marriage — and our childhood — quickly headed for darker days. It's hard to outrun the devastating force of generational trauma.

Even though my relationship with my mom was difficult during most of my childhood and adolescence, my mom loved me, as she loved all her children. I know this because I felt her steadfast ambition and dreams for a better life for all of us throughout my childhood.

She tells me I was so darling that it was so hard for her to stay mad at me. The way Mom talks about me as a toddler, it was like I was perfect in her eyes.

"Feeding you was a whole operation." Mom laughs

when telling me this story for the hundredth time. "I'd lay out newspaper all around your high chair before meals. Well, no matter what I did, you dug in and the food was everywhere! You'd fling it on the walls too!"

I also know that from the start, I tested Mom's limits and her patience. She'd tell me no and I'd look right in her eyes and do exactly what I'd been told not to do. It was like I was born a strong-willed child. During my toddler years I remember my defiance being received with both exasperation and a touch of pride. Spirited women ran in the family, after all.

I have many good memories with my family. Growing up in the country, west of Edmonton, Alberta — riding horses, playing outside till sundown, catching creepy-crawly critters and bringing them home to my mom, and even dumping a nest of caterpillars on my own head when my older cousin taunted that I wouldn't do it. My cousins and I used to chase and catch baby bunnies on my grandparents' farm and put them in plastic milk crates. Then we'd let them go, just to run around and catch them again. We'd do this all day long — unwittingly creating a generation of the fastest rabbits known to Parkland County.

In the summertime, my mom and her sisters would round up all the kids and take us to pick berries for jam. It was a multi-day ordeal. With buckets hanging from our necks (tied there by a thick string), we set off for hours of picking in the bush or at U-pick farms. Raspberries and saskatoons were abundant where we lived, and they were delicious! I ate more than I picked and always ended up with berry juice smeared across my face and hands.

I loved hunting for fresh eggs in the chicken coop and climbing the hay bales in the barn. My mom has a photo of me, when I'm probably around four years old, crouching down in rubber boots and a white cotton summer dress, proudly holding two fresh eggs in my hands. It's a picture that always fascinated me because I look so innocent and happy. I suppose I was. After all, I didn't know what lurked right around the corner.

THAT'S ALWAYS THE PROBLEM with revisiting my happy childhood memories. These beautiful moments are the truth, but they are not the whole truth. They are like a glittering collection of beautiful gems plucked from a pile of dark and smouldering coals. And the other memories in that much larger pile are menacing and dangerous. They burn and blister when disturbed. It's not just me — my family members feel the scorch as well. Sometimes it feels easier and kinder to just leave those smoking memories alone, protecting myself and my loved ones with silence. But one thing I've learned over the years is that silence is a tool of violence used against our people for generations in the attempt to erase and eradicate us. I will not participate in our silencing and so I must begin with myself. I must begin as that small four-year-old in that white dress.

A short time after that photo was taken, after I'd turned five, a relative who was also five introduced me to a game called "sexy wexy." He started touching my privates and showing me his little boy parts.

One day, I told my dad about the game. One moment I was standing in front of him chatting, the next moment I was flying onto the couch behind me propelled by the force of my father's slap to my face. I held my cheek, tears streaming around my fingers, while Dad towered over me, his face furious. "Don't you ever play that game again!" His warning forced through grinding teeth, his finger in my face.

I was stunned that my father, whom I loved and admired, was so angry with me. I didn't understand what I'd done wrong. All I knew was that the game was bad and now I was bad for having played it. So bad that I deserved the violent wrath of the man who was my hero.

Dad's blow sent my internal compass spinning. Even though the game was never mentioned again, from that moment forward I knew I was "bad" even if I didn't know why. My father—who loved the wildest horse or meanest dog, always winning them over with his steadfast gentleness—had shown me exactly how unredeemable and unlovable I was.

A rage, like a fire, started inside. I felt an anger that I couldn't control and that led to temper tantrums and greater rebelliousness. I was no longer admired for my strong spirit. I morphed into the family troublemaker: defiant, unmanageable, not to mention dirty.

Meanwhile, the chaos at home was escalating. My parents loved each other but their relationship was destructive and toxic. Home life was a never-ending cycle of fighting, screaming, hitting, cursing, and name-calling. My father was an alcoholic and would disappear for days on end, leaving my frustrated my mother with the four of us: my sister, three years older than me, and later my two brothers, six and eight years younger.

Eventually my mom would end up driving around searching for her missing husband. I remember numerous trips when she'd pile us into the van to go driving around looking for my dad. Sometimes she'd find Dad at Al's Barbershop in west Edmonton drinking with his old-timer cowboy friends. Other times she might find him out with his horses somewhere. One trip in particular sticks out in my mind. I was about seven years old. It was early evening in the summer and Mom was driving us in her Toyota minivan up and down big hills and through several pastures. It felt like an adventure. We were hunting for Dad—where could he be? But I could feel the stress radiating off Mom so I prayed we'd find him soon. In the distance we saw a figure wearing a black cowboy hat. It was Dad! As we got closer, I could see that he was weaving and wobbling, and I knew that meant he was "drunk."

Mom pulled up and Dad ducked into a nearby outhouse. She followed him in, leaving the door swinging wide. From the car we could see Dad sitting there with his jeans around his ankles and we could hear every word that passed between them.

"Where have you been, Rick?" Mom seethed.

"I'm looking after my horses." Dad smirked.

"Why don't you go drink some more, Rick?" she said in a mocking voice, waving at him on the toilet. Their exchange quickly escalated into a screaming and swearing match until Mom finally left him there in the outhouse declaring there was no point bringing him home in that shape.

She was probably right. Things were usually worse when Dad was home. Their screaming matches often turned physical and try as I might, I was powerless to prevent them.

"Stop!" I cried, as Mom leaped towards Dad. He grabbed her earrings, ripping them from her lobes. Blood was dripping down her neck. "No! Stop!" I wedged myself between them, screaming, sobbing while my other siblings hid somewhere in the house.

Looking back on it now, I wonder if my attempts to intervene were in part because I truly believed it was my increased acting out that was making things worse at home—not the other way around. For most of my life, I believed that the fights were my fault. After all, that's why I had to be sent away, right?

I LANDED IN MY first foster home around the age of six.

I'll never forget the day Mom dropped me off. It was a cold, grey day. My auntie Felice was there to support my mom. All I knew was that I was going to live with another family from our church. I didn't know for how long, but part of me was curious, and even a bit excited about this new adventure. I also felt sad because I knew it was my fault that I had to leave. Mom said I was out of control and she had too much on her plate so she was giving me over to a family that she hoped could handle me.

We stood outside the Child and Family Services office, in a looming brick building in Spruce Grove. Mom bent down and took my shoulders in her hands.

"Brandi, you're going to live with another family for a little while, okay? It's going to be fun. Mommy needs you to go there, okay?" She started to cry, her tears rolling down her cheeks and splattering onto the concrete. I nodded, feeling the rise of fear in my throat at the sight of my mom so upset.

"You be a good girl. I love you."

She gave me a quick embrace, stood, and walked away, sobbing heavily in my aunt's steadying embrace.

I don't remember much about my time in the foster home. They were a nice family from our church. But my rage and anger still had no outlet; in fact, now the fire inside felt even more unmanageable. I continued to have temper tantrums and act out against authority. It didn't take long for me to be kicked out of that home too.

This started a cycle of me ping-ponging between my own home and foster homes—and later, group homes—that would last until I was eighteen. Every time I returned home, I would hope upon hope that this time it would work out. But it only got worse.

My defiant attitude was like a lightning rod for my mom's frustration and rage with her own life. I endured beatings and verbal abuse from my mother, who was unwittingly passing along her inheritance of trauma and violence to me. There are bloody encounters that I can clearly picture today, but I won't go into the details. My dad would sometimes choke me against the wall until I was close to passing out at the requests from my mother to "deal with me" when I was "out of control."

And so, before long I'd end up back in the system and with a new foster family. Each time, it seemed I was sent farther and farther away.

I don't recall any neglect or abuse in the foster homes, except one time when I was about ten. I was living with a family in Spruce Grove and my foster mother was like an angel. She was loving and sweet and I connected deeply with her. I lived there for a couple of years. There were still plenty of times when I'd have outbursts — almost always following a bad phone conversation with my mom or right after returning from a weekend home visit. Even during those brief visits at home, I lived in constant anticipation of the next crisis or being the target of my mother's rage. I was constantly on edge and would return to my foster homes a simmering cauldron of anger, anguish, and shame.

On this particular occasion, I had just returned from a home visit and I was screaming, crying, and not listening to my foster parents' requests to calm down for reasons I can no longer recall. I do remember, however, being in the upstairs hallway when my foster dad kicked me from behind and I went flying down the stairs. Just more proof that I made everyone around me worse.

Even though it was hard every time I visited home, I never stopped longing for my parents' love and attention.

There's one incident that stands out for me. It was just before I went to the foster family in Spruce Grove. I was around nine and living at home. I'd had asthma for a few years and from time to time it landed me in the hospital, but on this occasion, the attack was severe enough to prompt a frantic visit to the ER.

I can still hear the doctor shouting, "We have to get an IV in her, now!" They needed to give me steroids to help me breathe properly, but my veins weren't having it. The needles kept popping out so they decided to try putting an IV in my foot. The pain was excruciating. The nurses had to hold me down on the stretcher while I screamed for my mom and dad to help me.

Mom was crying and Dad looked powerless.

"Keep trying. Try that one," said a nurse, pointing to a vein, as I continued screaming on the gurney. The doctor kept trying. Poke. Poke. Poke. Each stab brought searing pain but I was no longer screaming. Asthma blocked my airways and I gasped and flopped like a fish at the bottom of a boat, eyes wide with panic.

The staff did end up getting a needle in, and I lived, obviously. But that's not the point of this story. The point is that I loved the hospital. Yes, you read that right.

Even with an experience like that, the hospital was one of my favourite places to be when I was a kid. Sure, I was on heavy medications and isolated in a breathing tent at times, but I was getting attention. Relatives would visit and bring gifts. Caring nurses were at my beck and call. And best of all, my parents were concerned and their focus was on *me*. It was better than the chaos of home and better than a foster home. (As an aside, about a year later, Mom put me on a plant-based supplement and I miraculously got better. She said she asked God to heal me and it worked! I haven't had an issue with asthma since.) As an adult I'm so grateful, but at the time, losing the focused attention I received in the hospital felt like I had lost the keys to paradise.

. . .

THROUGHOUT MY TUMULTUOUS CHILDHOOD, my imagination always ran free and fantastical. It was a good thing too because it gave me a break from my dismal reality. My fantasies often focused on how one day I'd become someone important.

I'm gonna be famous, I just know it, I would tell myself as I walked through wild grass as tall as I was near my parents' acreage during warm summer evenings. More often than not, I could hear Mom and Dad fighting in the distance, but I pretended I was miles away.

Maybe I'll be a singer, or an actor. I'm going to travel the world. And the world's gonna love me, I told myself. I danced in circles, making paths in the grass and hunting for wildflowers.

But those dreams of mine didn't take away how lonely I was. I craved someone, anyone, to connect with. I wore out the VHS tapes of my all-time favourite series, *Anne of Green Gables*. I loved Anne and just knew that she and I could have been bosom friends. She was dramatic and outspoken like me. I wasn't an orphan like her, but I did live with other families. She was determined, she was a writer, she was fiery — we were so much alike. The only difference was that even though she got into loads of trouble, she still won the hearts of everyone she encountered. I knew that Anne was only a fictional character, but I still found solace in and drew inspiration from her. Her life wasn't perfect but in the end things worked out. That gave me something to hope for, even if her story was pretend.

Then there was Elvis. If Kohkum was his biggest fan, I was his second biggest. I fell head over heels in love with him — his stunning looks, his charm, his voice, his unique style, and his impact on the world captivated me. I connected to the lonely soul I sensed in him. His fame was bigger than life, yet he was one of the most vulnerable people on the planet. Listening to his music helped me to express emotions that I otherwise didn't know how to. I would play his sad melodic songs on repeat when I needed to release my pent-up emotions. I would cry alone in my bedroom, not truly alone because Elvis's voice was there to hold me.

Finally, food was a powerful form of escape. I learned at a young age that a peanut-butter-and-honey sandwich helped when I was lonely or upset. Tasting that sweet, gooey goodness always brought instant joy, comfort, and relief. This habit of seeking solace from food turned destructive. It followed me into my preteen and teen years when I was in group homes — places where mistreatment was rampant and the need for instant soothing was heightened. It followed me home and was my comfort when my parents' marriage ended for good when I was fourteen. I began to struggle with my weight and bingeing. If I was a drug addict, I swear I'd be dead by now given how many times I've binged on food when going through a crisis. Breaking this addiction and learning healthy ways to deal with life is something I'm still working on. Bit by bit I'm healing and letting go of the grip of food addiction.

Bit by bit, we've all been healing over the years.

Dad did his level best to help me during the tough times in my adult life. He's taken me in after I've been evicted, provided cash to purchase vehicles when the beaters I was driving gave out. He showed his love to me by providing security for me — and later, for me and my kids — during the moments I could've ended up on the street. Although, speaking of my kids, he was never impressed when I turned up pregnant. He warmed up to each of them the moment they were born, though, and loves all of them deeply.

Dad is still handsome. At sixty-seven his jet-black hair has turned almost completely silver, giving him an air of wisdom and clout. He's still a hard worker as well. His hands are calloused from decades of working in construction and to this day he gets up before dawn, is the first one on the job site, and the last one to leave. But alcohol's grip on him has lasted a lifetime. In the years since my parents' divorce, my dad has steadily drowned his regrets with bottles of whisky.

Mom worked hard over the years to keep house and home together. Whether it was her various cleaning jobs, being a school liaison for inner-city Indigenous kids, or marketing the latest health products—Mom worked her butt off, and still does. She put my two younger brothers through years of hockey and served at concession stands at games to help with the costs.

My mother almost succumbed to the pull of alcohol as well. Sometime after the divorce, she went on a party streak to rival Kohkum's that lasted years. She always kept her jobs, her house in order, and food on the table, but on the weekends she was in the bars partying till sunrise. Eventually the partying slowed. She bought a customized Harley-Davidson motorcycle and poured her energy into that bike and connecting with the supportive motorcycling community that came with it.

It makes me happy to see Mom standing strong after all she's been through. She had to be in survival mode for pretty much her whole life. Surviving to provide, to cope, to raise kids on her own. Mom had her flaws, but her heart has always been for her kids and she never stopped striving to give us a good life and she passed that ambition on to her kids. I've always admired her for it.

Mom introduced me to the anchor to my soul: God. She encouraged me chase my dreams. She always knows the latest best personal development resources and inspirational teachings and she models tenacity and endurance. Her conversations, encouragement, and guidance throughout my adult life have been the catalyst for much of my success.

Life was crazy and turbulent growing up, but no matter how bad things got at home, love was always at the core of our family. My parents were just broken people doing their best with what they knew, like most of us do. That's what makes our family even more beautiful—because we don't have it all together. Our love was forged in the fires of imperfection. Our blood bonds are not ones that can be broken. Our forgiveness is part of our strength. Trauma has swept across our generations like wildfire but we are not knocked down. We are still standing.

- 3 -

Author's note: this chapter contains scenes of sexual
violence that may prove triggering to some readers.

IT WAS A SPUR-OF-THE-MOMENT thing. Rose, Shannon,
and I were standing outside on the street near the
group home where we lived, smoking cigarettes. It was
mid-winter, 1993, and I wore an ankle-length bright-
blue denim jacket with sneakers. It wasn't enough to
keep out the cold but I looked good.

Rose and Shannon were about two years older than
me, and at twelve that's a big deal. They were cooler
and wiser, and I looked up to them. I'd gotten to know
them over the several months we'd spent together at the
Yellowhead Youth Centre. Ours was the world of lost
kids who bonded over our troubled backgrounds and
time spent in the system.

"We only got ten minutes left," I reminded Shannon and Rose. Everything was regimented here. We'd earned unsupervised breaks with good behaviour, but the routine was getting mundane and we were all feeling kinda cagey.

"Let's get out of here," said Shannon. She was Caucasian with short dirty-blond hair and blue eyes. She took a long drag of her cigarette and smiled while looking me up and down as if challenging my reaction. She'd lived most of her young life in the foster care system as well, but she was hardened by it more than I was. She acted a lot older than fourteen.

"Come on, let's go find booze and get drunk," she urged Rose and me. "It'll be fun. We can stay with my friends, but we gotta leave right now!"

The thought of finding some fun was enticing. We were all sick of the confines of the system we lived in. The rules, the strict routines that dulled our adolescent curiosity, and the monotonous interactions with staff members. We craved adventure and the rush of the unknown.

All at once, we ran. I could see my breath in the crisp air and taste the thrill of freedom. The stucco-sided houses flew by as we galloped into the night. The longer we ran without stopping, the less chance the group home staff would catch us. The allure of the hustle and bustle of downtown Edmonton drew us closer. There was so much world to be discovered!

This was the first time I took off from this group home, although I'd run away from others in the same way. There was never any plan in place, we'd just crash on the sofas of friends, or wander the city until we were tracked down and returned. Then we'd have to earn the right to unsupervised breaks again and once we did, well, it wasn't long till we took off again.

But this wasn't a random foray into the city. Rose and Shannon knew exactly where we were going. They were both streetwise and knew their way around. I was just an impressionable country kid compared to them. Everything was still so new and exciting to me. I thought the goal was to somehow find money to buy booze and party and I couldn't wait to let loose, forget our troubles, and act like giddy girls together. At last, I was one of the cool kids.

After about half an hour we arrived at a high-rise apart-ment in downtown Edmonton right next to the luxurious Fairmont Hotel Macdonald. I was impressed. How did they know someone in this part of town? I might not know much, but I knew that all the celebrities stayed at the Hotel Macdonald with its concierges and bellmen in suits, and fancy cars and limos lined up outside.

But the building we went into was not luxurious. It was rundown and smelled like moulding carpet. To my surprise, Shannon and Rose walked right into an apartment and I followed them with an expectant grin on my face, eager to unwind and party, just the three of us, like we'd planned. It was small with a kitchen to the right and an open living room sparsely furnished with a small TV and a 1980s-style brown couch. Cigarette smoke crawled across the apartment like a snake.

A man in his late twenties sat smoking on the couch leaning over a long brown coffee table with an over-flowing ashtray on it. He got up and warmly greeted Shannon with a hug, motioning us to come in. The warmth inside felt good compared to the bitter cold. Another man, also older than us, walked into the room.

"You wanna smoke?" he asked, handing a pack to Shannon and offering one to us all.

He seemed friendly and charming enough, but I sensed something was off. Suddenly the second man asked me to follow him to the bedroom. I wanted to be cool in front of my friends, so I acted like it was nothing. Nothing, to go into a bedroom with a stranger who was more than twice my age. The man had jet-black skin, a twinkling white smile, and spoke in broken English.

He took me into a dark bedroom with two twin beds. He towered over me like a shadow. I was five foot one and maybe a hundred and fifteen. A sudden menacing look formed in his eyes. He pushed me onto the bed and crawled on top of me. I yelled out for help, but no one answered. Where were Shannon and Rose? I could hear them giggling. The pain was excruciating as he ripped my virginity away. I think I had an out-of-body experience because it was like I was watching it happen while hovering above that bed with him on top of me.

AFTER HE LEFT, I stumbled to the bathroom, sobbing. I clasped my arms around my heaving chest. My thoughts were scrambled and my limbs began to quake as my body went into shock. My eyes cut to the toilet bowl. A bloody condom floated on the top of the water, staining it red. In that moment, I understood with perfect clarity that this was the exact worth of my innocence, my body, my life—nothing more than nasty trash waiting to be flushed away.

There was laughter coming from the living room. It was as if no one had a clue about what had just happened—or they just didn't care. Whichever it was, I knew for certain that I was in this situation alone.

Whimpering, I slapped cold water on my face and pulled myself together. I didn't want to show any fear in case I'd be the target of more violence. Showing my best tough front, I joined Shannon and Rose in the living room where they were having drinks with both men and treating them like old-time pals. The one who had just raped me was parading around like a king, yet whenever he looked at me, he sneered in disgust.

We didn't leave the apartment that night. Or the next. Fear and shock were playing tricks with my mind. I felt betrayed by Shannon and Rose, but I knew I had to stay friendly. I was terrified they would take off and leave me there.

When we did leave, it wasn't of our own volition. The second or third night we were herded down to the underground car park and moved to another apartment on the other side of the city.

Another man claimed me and raped me several times. I didn't fight back or yell because I knew no one would help. I spent most of my time in a corner of a small bedroom with my knees pulled up towards my face. I think I was there about a week but it was difficult to tell. The curtains were always drawn so I never knew if it was day or night.

Shannon and Rose on the other hand seemed to be

having a great time. They hung out with the men in the rest of the apartment, drinking, smoking, talking — it was like they were all friends. Nothing made sense. Along with confusion, guilt hit hard. I thought everything was my fault because I ran away and put myself in danger. Who would come looking for me? Who would even care? I was just a runaway from a child-welfare system that was already overloaded. But I didn't want to die. I prayed to God and begged forgiveness. *Please help me. Can you send your angels to rescue me?*

My prayer sparked something in me, almost as if the tiniest fissure of light made its way into my heart, kindling my courage. There had to be a way out. I took a deep breath and as quietly as I could, I ventured out into the hallway. I could hear the voices of everyone else floating down the hall from the living room. My heart was banging like a drum and I prayed no one would hear me. I cracked a door and peeked inside. It was another bedroom, empty, but I could see a phone on the bedside table. I slipped inside, picked up the phone, and dialed the first number that came to mind.

"Hello?" The voice of my kohkum on the other end instantly steadied me.

I didn't tell her I was in danger. I just asked if I could come to visit.

"Well, of course you can come see me, my Brandi," she said. "You're always welcome here, you know that."

It's difficult to explain what happened next.

Emboldened by the brief call with my kohkum, I marched out of the bedroom, down the hall, and into the living room, where I put on the show of my life. What I said exactly, I've never been able to remember, but it was something along the lines of how something urgent had come up with my kohkum and I had to quickly visit her (glossing over *how* I'd learned this from my bedroom prison), but then I'd come right back to the apartment with them. I was enthusiastic about this last point. Yes, of course I'd return. I didn't even want to leave in the first place. It's just such a fun place to be!

They bought it.

I'll pause to let you take that in.

They bought my story and agreed to take me to my kohkum's for a quick visit. My prayer of thanks coursed through my entire little body. But I wasn't out of danger yet. One of the men agreed to drive me. This time I was alone as he brought me into the parking garage and made me sit in the front with him. It was a long dreadful ride. The car was an Oldsmobile of some kind with tinted windows and a blue interior. It was dark and freezing outside and I didn't know if he was taking me to my kohkum's or whether he was actually planning on killing me. I figured it was equal odds. But I had a strong instinct that I needed to keep up the happy act. If I slipped and let my terror show, or allowed a tear to escape down my cheek, I knew it could set him off. My mind was racing, my heart was palpitating out of my chest, but I prayed for the strength to maintain my calm exterior.

After what seemed like an eternity, he pulled up in front of my kohkum's house and stopped the car. He flashed a smile my way and his white teeth shimmered in the dark. One tooth was missing and he slithered his tongue through it continuously. He turned and leaned towards me and I forced myself not to jump. I wasn't out of the car yet, he could still just speed off again. But he didn't touch me. He reached past me and opened the glove compartment. He showed me the collection of knives inside, and implied what would happen if I didn't return. I gripped the door handle and nodded in agreement.

And then I was out of the car, bolting for the safety of Kohkum's ground-floor apartment. I ripped open her front door and once inside, I locked it and stood with my back against the door for a minute, gasping with relief. Then I went into Kohkum's kitchen, where she was waiting. Seeing Kohkum's face, smelling the warmth of her home, and feeling the embrace of her loving arms, I felt as if I had a second chance at life.

I didn't tell her what had happened to me, and she didn't ask. She knew I'd been missing for about a week, but I'd gone missing before and Kohkum's code was that everyone could keep the secrets they wanted to keep. She didn't pry. She didn't interfere. She loved.

I slept with her in her bed that night. I suppose I should have been afraid that the man was still waiting for me outside. Perhaps he was going to break in and drag me back. But the truth is, I wasn't afraid. The moment I got into Kohkum's arms I simply knew they couldn't touch me anymore. Like I said, to me, Kohkum was indestructible. But I wasn't. I had to pull a pillow over my head to block out horrifying flashbacks that bombarded me all night long and I hoped I wouldn't wake my kohkum with my uncontrollable shaking.

A couple of days later, staff from the group home showed up to collect me. My kohkum eventually had to report that I'd been found. Incidentally, Shannon and Rose never returned to that particular group home.

I had all my privileges stripped from me and was confined to my room for several days because I had run away. I hated being locked away with the traumatic memories of everything I had just experienced, but I liked being left alone to sleep all day. Sleep was the only escape left to me.

About a week later I plopped myself down on the plastic chair in the staff office for my regular meeting with my caseworker, Kelly. She'd been nice enough to me from time to time and I was desperate for an adult I could trust, so I decided to open up to her.

"I was hurt," I told her, head down, and hands tightly clasped in my lap. She didn't respond. I looked up and stared across the cluttered desk where she was seated. Behind her the wall was busy with clippings, schedules, miscellaneous printouts, and calendar pages. Kelly had taken my thick file from the enormous leaning stack on her desk and was flipping through it, almost listlessly. Then she picked up a pen and started charting the daily schedules. I tried again. "You know . . . I was raped . . ." My face turned beet red and I felt large beads of sweat spring to my forehead and start rolling down into my eyebrows. I wiped my face and hung my head lower.

Kelly put down the pen and looked at me for the first time. I couldn't meet her gaze but found myself holding my breath and begging myself not to cry. "Well, Brandi," she finally said, "that's what happens when you take off. Don't do it again."

So there I had it. I'd shared the most horrific thing that had ever happened to me and it was professionally confirmed that I'd brought it on myself. I left her office that day feeling like I'd been ground so deeply into the dirt that I'd never be able to get up again. I was no good. I was dirty. No one would ever want me.

- 4 -

SOMETHING CHANGED IN ME after the rape. The rage was back, tenfold, and it roared through my body, threatening to consume me if I didn't release it into the world. But no matter how much I let it out, the intense fires of my anger would never abate and I felt as though I was burning alive. I defied authority on every occasion possible. I broke every rule forced on me, picked fights, and seethed with disrespect around most adults.

The Yellowhead Youth Centre had a Time Out Room for the kids who acted up or threatened to harm themselves. It was a small, empty room, painted entirely white with locks on the outside of the door. I was put in there several times to "cool off" when my temper got out of hand. There was a reinforced-glass window for staff so they could keep an eye on the Time Out Room's occupants while they worked. I could see Kelly's desk from in there.

I remember the first time they used restraints on me. I was angry and cursing and not following orders to calm down and go to my room. The next thing I knew I was tackled from behind and knocked to the ground by a worker named Darren. His heavy body was on top of me and I felt him putting the restraints on and something snapped. I fought for my life — kicking, punching, clawing, and screaming. I was back in that dark bedroom. I was powerless and in danger.

My mind roared. *This time I will fight! This time I won't let him hurt me!*

But I was no match for Darren's bulk and he pinned me until I relented and stopped struggling. Men, it seemed, only get off you when you are good and broken. A crowd of kids and staff members had gathered to watch the show. No one had moved a muscle to intervene or uttered a word in protest. I was hauled from the floor in restraints and thrown into a padded room for punishment.

Restraints became their go-to for dealing with me. After each one of these of episodes, I would get written up, be marched into a therapy room to have a heart-to-heart talk with some Kelly-clone about lessons I'd learned, and then trudge on, following their mindless routines until my next outburst.

This was how the months bled into each other as I bounced from one group home to another, each one punctuated by failed attempts to move back home with my family. I can no longer remember distinguishing details about the homes or even how many I stayed in. Although there is one place that still burns in my mind all these years later.

I was thirteen, and going into another group home. I was devastated that my attempt to live at home had ended so soon. My dad was the one who drove me to the new home. My mom didn't come along for the ride as we'd just gotten into a major fight and I'd been on the receiving end of every no-good name in the book. When Dad pulled up to the building, he threw his truck into park and turned to me. It was winter and already dark outside but I could see that he held something in his hand.

"Here, my girl, you take these with you." His eyes were wet and his words were choked with emotion as he pressed his gold wedding ring and a small ivory wolf carving into my palm. "When you have these, it means I'm with you. So you don't have to feel scared or alone. Okay?"

I nodded silently and clutched them with all my might.

When I arrived at the group home a worker saw them and confiscated them immediately. He told me that we were not allowed to have anything of value in our rooms, so they would be locked in a special cabinet for safety. I was hysterical to keep them but he pried them out of my hands. I cried myself to sleep that night, curled up on the top bunk in a room I shared with three other girls.

Not long after, I asked to see my treasures. No one knew what I was talking about. There was no special cabinet for valuables. The staff member who took them from me acted as if I made it all up. They believed him of course. I was gutted.

I grew colder and tougher.

And I kept running away.

Sometimes people act surprised to hear that I ran away from the group homes after the horrific experience I had outside them. But the group homes weren't safe. My home wasn't safe. Running was as safe as staying, minus the authority I so loathed.

I ran once with a good friend, Buffy, from one of the group homes. She was fifteen, which was two years older than me at the time. I saw her as my wiser, prettier, and much cooler older sister. She, in turn, took me on like a little sister.

When we ran away from the group home it was just for the adventure of it. For several days I tagged along and couch surfed with her as she visited friends and family on the north side of Edmonton. This was when I discovered that she had a drug habit. A serious one. The kind that required needles.

I was completely naive to hardcore drugs and their effects. I idolized Buffy and was willing to try anything, including getting high. I begged her to hook me up, but she kept giving me a firm no. She wouldn't budge.

"Look, little sis," she said in exasperation. "There is no way I'm going to let you put anything in your arm, so drop it already!"

I was upset because I didn't understand the implications and had no idea that she was looking out for me. I thought she was just treating me like a little kid.

The next night she took me to a drug house downtown, although I didn't know that's what it was. As far as I knew, we were visiting a friend of hers, drinking a few beers, and playing cards in his rundown kitchen. This "friend" turned out to be an old man, probably in his sixties, balding, with a wife-beater tank top on, and a big, hairy gut.

We drank and played cards for a while and I ended up falling asleep on the couch. I woke in the night and looked around for Buffy. I could see a light coming from the bedroom. The door was ajar and through it I could see Buffy having sex with that disgusting old man. When he was finished, he rolled off her and handed Buffy a needle. She hungrily tied off her arm and shot the murky liquid into her vein. Her eyes rolled back and she slumped forward, motionless. The man propped her back up on the bed and promptly passed out as well.

I could taste bile in the back of my throat. There was my beautiful friend bartering her young body to this old pervert. We left the next day but my heart was no longer in the adventure. I told Buffy, but she wanted to keep moving, so we went our separate ways. I called my dad to come pick me up. He was relieved to hear my voice but horrified at the part of town I was in. He rushed to get me—despite the late hour—and brought me home. The social worker was out the next day to bring me back to the group home.

A FEW MONTHS LATER, I was on the run again. I'd found a boyfriend at this point. He lived in the city and was sixteen years old, which made me feel pretty grown up for a thirteen-year-old. One day he called and offered to come pick me up for a little road trip. I was in! He and his friends swung by that night. High on love and anticipating adventure, I jumped in the car.

We headed to Camrose, which was a couple hours away. Glen, my boyfriend, had told me they had borrowed the car, but it turned out to be stolen. We pulled up to a darkened house.

"My mom's friend just bought this place," Glen announced, sliding out of the car. "It's vacant right now though." I jumped out after him and followed him to the front porch. Within moments he'd forced his way into the house.

The three of us hung out there for a few days, drinking, smoking, and acting like punk kids. Then, maybe out of boredom, I'm not sure, Glen dared me to do a B&E.

"It's easy. You just go inside, be as fast as you can, and take what you can find," he said when he saw me hesitating. "Come on, don't be a wuss."

I didn't want Glen to be disappointed in me and the more we talked about it, the better it sounded. We'd pawn or sell whatever I got and use the money to drive west to the mountains to hide out for a bit. It was a pretty good plan. I agreed to do it.

They drove to a neighbourhood nearby. It was broad

daylight. They pulled up in a back alley behind a brown two-storey house. They assured me no one was home. Glen turned, looked at me, and smiled a challenging sort of grin. Then he just stared at me, waiting to see what I would do, as if this was some sort of test of my love and commitment to him. Not that he needed to test me, I would have done anything to please him. I got out, heart thumping against the back of my throat, and headed over to the house.

The door was unlocked, so I opened it and went up the stairs to the main-floor hallway. I had no idea what I was doing, so I just started looking around for valuables. I was opening up drawers and cabinets, when a guy walked out of one of the bedrooms. I looked at him, horrified, and bolted for the door as fast as I could run. I jumped into the waiting car, hollering "Go, go, go!!" We squealed out of the alley but not quickly enough. The man caught the car's licence plate and a couple weeks later the police arrived to arrest me and the others.

I'd levelled up from group home detention centres to the real deal—I was sentenced to serve six months in the Edmonton Young Offender Centre (EYOC).

Life at the group homes may have been tough, but it was a cakewalk compared to jail. Jail was awful—humiliating strip searches, daily harassment, and solitary confinement were just a few of the ways they institutionalized the torture of the young people within their walls. The first time I refused to go to my cell and mouthed off at a staff member I was put in a "time-out room" next to the control desk. I banged on the doors and kicked at the walls while yelling insults to staff through the small viewing slit in the door. A jail guard showed up and shackled my hands together. I was led off the ward to the solitary confinement area. He pushed me inside—that should shut me up and make me listen.

It was an empty, cold concrete cell. I had only a thin blanket and a small barred window to look out of. Being alone for hours that turned into days was torturous. Oh, the nightmares I had there. They seemed to be ripped right from the pages of Kohkum's doomsday sermons with their white crosses dripping blood, hellfires, and souls burning in anguish. There were no lights to turn on for comfort. I felt like I was surrounded by demons and the residual torments of all the other children who had languished in this cell before me.

When I wasn't in solitary confinement, I was assigned a cell that I shared with my roommate Sam. She was a big Cree girl who'd already done plenty of stints in juvie and it was assumed by most that she'd continue this pattern right into the adult prison system. At first, I was scared of her. She was stocky and tough and no one wanted to mess with her. But soon enough, we connected and became friends. Where she was large and quietly menacing, I was small, insecure, and mouthy. She looked out for me and I idolized her. To pass time in our cell Sam and I would swap stories from our childhoods and life on the outs. Her tales of growing up on the Saddle Lake Cree Nation were much worse than my turbulent childhood. I shuddered at the detailed accounts of beatings, poverty, and hardship that she shared and thought how good I had had it in comparison.

Sam and I went our separate ways in life but reconnected on social media some years ago. She had a couple of kids and battled with addiction. She struggled to be the mom she wanted to be. She would get straight in an attempt to give them all a better life, but she'd then fall back into the gaping hole of trauma at the centre of her being. About five years ago, Sam died after a battle with cancer. She'd never managed to break the cycle of addiction, never managed to realize a life that wasn't suffering and struggle. Never managed to live free.

I also met a boy named Clayton during my stay in

EYOC. We attended coed classes together. He was fifteen and took a romantic interest in me. He was Cree, dark, strikingly handsome, and well-respected in jail. He was smart and philosophical, but I was oblivious to his attraction to me. I'd broken up with Glen and didn't have boys on my mind at the time, I guess. Then one day during English class, Clayton made his move. He sat on the desk in front of me and leaned in towards me. Then he held my gaze with a playful, knowing look and winked. It startled me and my face blushed red. If he was fishing, I was hooked.

We began passing little folded-paper love letters to each other during class. We poured our lonely hearts into those letters, sharing our pasts with each other and our dreams for the future. He'd lost his mother early, and just like every native child I met who'd been through the foster care system, his stories of trauma and turbulence were hair-raising. Our letters turned romantic and we vowed a love that would last forever, beyond the steel bars of our captivity. Sometimes, during class changes when the halls were swarming with students, Clayton would grab my arm and pull me aside to steal a kiss. It was a thrilling way to help pass the time.

When we were back in the real world, our relationship didn't last long. We both had tumultuous home lives and it was hard enough trying to walk on the straight and narrow myself, let alone helping him do the same. He told me he wanted a family one day, to be free of all the turmoil, but in the end, he couldn't shake the clutches of his past trauma. For a few years, we'd talk on the phone here and there, still promising our undying love. He even made a visit to my kohkum's house. She did the obligatory run-down of asking him who he was and where he was from and then welcomed him warmly, as she did everyone. It was a special visit for all of us and one that still brings a smile to my face whenever I remember it. Eventually, though, Clayton and I lost contact. About ten years ago, I learned he'd hanged himself in a hotel, unable to outrun his demons. The news of his death left me feeling gutted, empty, and sad.

DURING MY TIME IN jail, I befriended another girl named Samantha, but she was the polar opposite of my room-mate Sam. Samantha was mixed Asian-Cree, baby-faced, bubbly, and popular. She was seasoned when it came to life in jail. Seeing that I was a newbie, she went out of her way to befriend me. Her stature was small but her laughter was huge and infectious. She could whisk us all away with her stories, and for a moment, we would be outside of that jail and free from our collective misery. No wonder everyone wanted to be around Samantha.

A few years later, Samantha hanged herself as well. Another young, beautiful, broken soul lost in tragedy.

WHEN I WALKED OUT of that jail, six months — and a lifetime — later, I pledged to turn my life around. I'd had my fill of the life I'd been living. I knew that the odds were against me — just as they are against every Indigenous child caught up in the riptide of the colonialist institutions that have been systematically eradicating them for generations. But with everything that had happened to me in just thirteen short years, I knew I would be dead before I could live thirteen more. I had to try.

One final note. A few years ago, I learned that Buffy was found murdered in a hotel room in Edmonton. We'd lost touch over the years, but I'd never forgotten her kindness and protective care. My heart aches thinking of how she left this world — abused and used. My precious Cree sister reduced to a newspaper clipping, like so many who have met the same end. No one was ever arrested for her murder, but whoever her killer was, he could never have known the treasure he'd stolen from the world. He'd never have known that good and gentle heart that he'd stilled forever. No doubt all he saw was just another disposable Indian — trash to dump in the river or flush down the toilet.

Buffy's pretty smile flashes through my memories from time to time and her death haunts my soul. Sometimes I wonder how it was that I survived when so many did not. It's an impossible question, but it infuses my life with grief, guilt, and gratitude.

I'm humbled by the fact that I still have my life — and I refuse to waste it. My voice is not one that will be snuffed out because I carry the conviction that we must get justice for Sam, for Samantha, for Clayton, for Buffy, and for the countless others, so that no more will be lost.

- 5 -

LIVING THE STRAIGHT AND narrow was a bit of a hit-and-miss experiment, but at least I wasn't living as wildly as I had before. At fourteen, I moved in with my dad, who got his own apartment after the divorce. I think we both desperately hoped that we could both make a clean start at life, but he still struggled with his drinking, I still struggled with my anger, and there were still plenty of family storms to rock the boat of our tentative stability.

One memory that stands out for me was an occasion when my mom called me at Dad's apartment. She was distraught and told me she felt abandoned and wanted to die. This was so unlike her that I was immediately terrified. I got a ride to her house and rushed in, scared of what I would find. She was in her PJs, crying on the floor of her bedroom and holding a half-empty bottle of pills. The other half was already working its way through her system. I wrestled the pills out of her hands while she sobbed and then collapsed in a heap. I helped her get on her feet and back into bed, where she lay weeping while I stroked her hair. I knew how she felt. The crushing responsibility of life often felt too heavy for my shoulders too. I just dealt with it differently.

That night I went on a partying bender, desperate to dance, smoke, and drink myself into oblivion. And then the next night. And the next. My partying led to hanging with the "bad kids" at school, but when I got kicked out of grade ten for smoking a joint on school property, I shaped up again.

FOR THE NEXT FEW years, I was quite a goody-goody. I was insecure and a loner in high school. I didn't know how to properly socialize with the kids who had "normal" upbringings and I didn't think anyone wanted to be friends with me anyway.

I had a bit of a disastrous unrequited crush on a boy named Dallas that distracted me for a little while, but for the most part I kept to myself and tried to concentrate on passing my classes. I was back at another foster home for most of high school but when Dad moved to a townhouse in the city during my last semester of grade twelve, I joined him there.

Dad was drinking heavily as usual. He'd go to work every day, then drink himself into oblivion with whisky at night. Dad was always sad and when he got drunk, he'd pour out his woes and confess to me that he didn't want to live his life anymore. The pressure of dealing with another suicidal parent was more than I could bear. I prayed all the time, begging God to save my dad, because I sure couldn't. Every day while riding the bus home from school I'd have to fight the rising panic in my mind. *Would I find Dad hanging in the basement?*

I did everything I could to try to make Dad happy. I thought that if I excelled in school he would be encouraged. But he didn't seem to notice. What about if I became highly successful? Then he might snap out of it.

Singing was always something I was good at and I liked doing it as well. I sang solos in church as a kid and the warmth and acceptance I felt from a crowd helped to quell some of the emptiness inside. I'd been taking singing lessons and my teacher had been encouraging me to perform in public. I decided right then and there that I would have a career as a country music singer.

I poured my energy into arranging singing gigs wherever I could. I quickly worked my way up and found myself in demand at the local rodeo circuits singing the national anthem and performing the halftime shows. I'd get decked out in flashy cowgirl gear with skin-tight Wrangler jeans and a peekaboo midriff. Then I'd curl my dark hair so it bounced when I walked, and paint my face like a dazzling movie star. People told me I was a head-turner, and I delighted in the attention and adoration I received. All of it just made me more determined to make it big in the music world.

I landed a management team who dubbed me "Little Miss Dynamite." Soon, I was well on my way to securing a record deal. Suddenly I'd found a purpose — I could reach people through music. I channelled my broken heart into those honky-tonk songs and broke the hearts of everyone listening. Then I'd turn around and soothe everyone's pain and inspire them for better days. Everyone but Dad, that is.

Dad didn't snap out of his own heartaches and his self-destructive agony began to take a toll on me. At one point I finally lost it. I was on my bedroom floor sobbing my eyes out, the full deal — heaving, hollering, and lamenting my frustration like a full-force gale. God was getting the brunt of it. Why wasn't He helping my dad? Did He even hear my prayers? What was it going to take for a breakthrough? I'd tried everything!

My dad came home and yelled from downstairs asking me what was wrong. He thought someone had died. I couldn't share any of it with him, so I stayed in my room and cried myself to sleep. When I woke up, something in me had broken. The burden of trying to make my dad better was too much. My prayers weren't working, my growing stardom meant nothing. Little Miss Dynamite was burnt-out. Officially. I returned to the only other way of dealing with the world that I knew: living wild and living hard.

In a span of a few months, I'd ditched my singing career, dropped out of school, and began using a fake ID to get into bars. Those months were a fog of drunkenness, parties, and one-night stands. I was numbing out. If I couldn't beat 'em, I might as well join 'em. I'd use the very things I hated the most to drown out my anguish: booze and predatory men.

The men I hooked up with could smell my vulnerability from miles away, like sharks can smell blood in the water. The bars were swarming with them and I'm shocked that I was never a victim of violence or left for dead in a ditch somewhere. I could have been because I remember very few of those sexual encounters.

After four months of stumbling around, I learned I was pregnant. I wasn't even entirely sure who my baby's father was. It was enough to jerk me back into reality. Hard.

I was going to be a mom at eighteen. Me, the person who had never felt like she belonged anywhere or to anyone for most of her life. Well, I was going to make sure my baby belonged — even if I didn't have a dime to my name or a stable place to call home.

So help me God.

ON APRIL 23, 1999, my daughter was born on a warm, cloudless morning in west Edmonton.

She was beautiful: tiny and calm with ten perfect little fingers and toes. I held her and explored her perfection in awe. Here was my darling baby, she was mine and I was hers, and I whispered a vow into her rosebud ear that I would protect her for all time.

The spell was broken by a stern-looking nurse. "We've found a private room and we are going to move you and the baby there for your protection. We've put a bassinet in there so she'll stay with you for the time being."

For just one glorious moment, I had totally forgotten that I was locked up in a psych ward.

I'd been there for almost half my pregnancy. Perhaps it was the intense pressure of the impending responsibility of motherhood, without a partner, or even a home, that had caused me to crack. I don't know. But about five months into the pregnancy, I fell into psychosis. It was a terrifying ordeal of hallucinations, spiritual visions, confusion, and detachment from reality. The psych ward became my temporary home for the final months of my pregnancy with the occasional weekend stay at Mom's.

I had no time, mentally, emotionally, or physically, to prep for my daughter's arrival because I was lost to the terror-scape of psychosis right up until the birth of my daughter. The symptoms went away immediately after she was born, but doctors kept me in hospital a few weeks afterwards for monitoring.

So, there we were — the two of us in a steel room in the psych ward. I had nothing to my name and I was bringing her into a world of uncertainty, but she was my darling and I was going to fight to give her a good life. I named her Faith.

We went to live with my mom after being released. She adored her first grandchild, but as usual, things were volatile between Mom and me. It didn't take long for us to start back into the war of the wills and within a few months, baby and I got the boot. So I packed up Faith and our meagre belongings and went to live with my kohkum for a spell.

I wish the next part of my story was that my overwhelming love for Faith was enough to heal all my festering wounds and that I shaped up and became the mom she deserved. But this isn't a fairy tale, this is real life. And I am a person who tells true stories, no matter how much they hurt.

I'm not sure what got into me, but I started neglecting Faith little by little. I would leave her in a dirty diaper too long or not sanitize her bottles correctly. My fierce burning love was being smothered under a heavy blanket of numb despair. Before long, I was mindlessly chasing the escape, back to partying, back to my own bottle. And before long, I wasn't just neglecting Faith, I was failing to protect her.

One night, I was drinking at Kohkum's house with a friend while Kohkum was out partying elsewhere. Faith was only a few months old. We had invited a couple of guys over and we all partied in the kitchen for a couple hours while I left Faith in the baby swing in the living room. I passed out upstairs afterwards. It was my friend who brought my crying baby to me and woke me up. How I ever could've done that to my innocent child is beyond me. I get choked up when I think of that incident.

My mom and sister came to visit me one day. When they saw the conditions that we were living in, they placed a call to Child and Family Services. The next thing I knew, Faith was taken away and placed in a foster home. The generational cycle was repeating itself and I was lost in the depths of its tidal pulls. Whenever I would surface from my intoxication, I'd drown in my despair and self-hatred.

In the meantime, Mom was working with the foster system and managed to get custody of Faith. Somewhere deep inside I felt the sting of her not having protected me when I was child, along with gratitude that she was sheltering my precious Faith. I drank to block both of these feelings.

I was that reckless twelve-year-old again. Unlovable, unredeemable, trash to be used and disposed of. I woke up countless mornings in motels I didn't remember going to, with men I didn't remember meeting — my body bearing the bruises and the blood of their harsh use of me.

When Faith was four months old, I found out I was pregnant again, and I didn't know for certain who the father was. Again. And once again, pregnancy provided a wake-up and shape-up call for me. As much as I appreciated that Kohkum would always offer me a roof over my head, she could not offer me a stable home. Her house was party central and her door was open to any and all who needed a place to crash. If I was going to find my feet, I'd need a steadier base. So I moved back to my mom's temporarily and got busy repairing my relationship with both her and Faith.

Before too long, I was able to secure subsidized housing for single moms along with funding for daycare and I moved into a rented one-bedroom home in Stony Plain. It was scary going it alone with one baby and another on the way, but I was determined to try for the sake of my growing family.

IN MAY 2000, MY son Luke was born. He gazed at me with his beautiful clear blue eyes and my heart overflowed with adoration for him. Once again, I vowed to my child that I would do everything in my power to give him a better life than I had.

But my God, life with a one-year-old and a newborn was rough. I felt lonely, exhausted, and directionless most of the time. A couple of weeks after Luke was born, I turned on the radio and heard my friend Adam

Gregory singing. I had toured with him a bit when we were both early in our singing careers. He went on to sign a recording contract with Sony Music Canada. I went on to ... what? I went on to mindless partying and now I was alone and a single mom.

I sank to my knees in tears. I thought music was going to save me from a life of despair, but I'd sure managed to destroy those dreams in a hurry. Now I had no dreams at all. I was nineteen and my life was over. I felt the grip of despair tightening around my throat. What was the point of even staying alive?

Luke's cries startled me back to reality. He was the point. Faith was the point. I got up off the floor. I had to keep it together somehow. My babies needed me. And they needed me to find some dreams again.

Despite feeling worthless and rotten, I caught hold of that thread of finding another dream. I wrapped my fist around the possibility that one day I could still make an impact on the world, and vowed to hang on. I felt a small current of hope simmer down that line and thanked God I was a natural dreamer. I knew this would be a light that would guide me from this dark place. Step by small step. But I still had a long way to go.

- 6 -

"STEVEN" CAME INTO MY life when I was twenty-one. He was a groomsman at a friend's wedding I was attending and he'd come all the way up from Manitoba for the occasion. He was kind, shy, and the drunkest one at the party. I was immediately drawn to him. Also, he didn't try to just get in my pants. That was a shocker for me because that's what I'd been used to from men up to this point.

Our connection was instant and our relationship bloomed quickly. Within months, I was packing up my apartment and hitting the road with my two toddlers to join Steven two provinces away in Altona, Manitoba.

At first, I was head over heels in love with my new boyfriend, and thrilled that my dreams for a better life for me and my kids were finally coming to pass. But it didn't take long to realize that Steven was a stumbling alcoholic who drank every minute he wasn't working at a mechanics shop in town. My burning love turned to ashes and my dreams to disappointment.

To keep my spirits up, I decided to explore another dream that had long pulled at my heart — writing professionally. Since I was stuck in Altona, I figured it was as good a place as any to start. I went to the office of the local community newspaper, the *Red River Valley Echo*, and asked to meet with the editor, Deborah. The next thing I knew I was sitting across from her trying to convince her to give me a position with the paper. I was nervous. I had no experience outside a love of writing, unless you counted the stacks of diaries I had written over the years. (I didn't think she would.) But I did have an eagerness to learn the ropes of newspaper reporting and a willingness to take any job they'd be willing to throw my way.

I guess it was enough because Deborah offered me a part-time reporting gig. I was thrilled! My first assignment was a play at the elementary school. I felt sophisticated and important strolling in with my borrowed camera and notebook, pretending I knew what I was doing.

I didn't have a computer at home, so I wrote the

story by hand and had to go into the office to type it out. I spent hours on my story, my two fingers pecking at the keyboard like a couple of chickens because I also didn't know how to type. But I pulled it off and got my first story published for a whopping fifty bucks. When I saw my byline printed for the first time I freaked out and showed everyone I knew.

For about eight months I flourished and developed my storytelling skills. Deborah took me under her wing and provided guidance and offered opportunities for growth that I am forever grateful for. I loved everything about the job, from meeting new people to reporting on stories, not to mention the sense of worth and pride that it gave me.

But things at home continued to disintegrate as Steven's drinking grew more out of control. For the sake of my children and my sanity, I had to end things, even though it also meant the end of a job I loved more than anything else I'd ever done.

Once again, it was my dad who came to my rescue, pulling a U-Haul behind his truck for the almost three-thousand-kilometre round trip to take my kids and me home to Alberta. But I'd left my job, my home, and my heart in Manitoba. I truly came back to nothing. I moved into public housing in south Edmonton and needed welfare assistance as jobs that would allow me to care for my two young children and meet our basic living needs just didn't exist. I went to the food bank more times than I can count during those years. My kids used to think it was a big adventure to go and see the neat stuff we would get in our food hampers. They didn't realize we were poor and they didn't see the heaviness I was carrying. They were just excited to get fruit, snacks, and brand-name cookies.

I chased a couple dead-end relationships and had a few meaningless flings. They brought a momentary sense of connection that I craved but, in the end, they always left me empty. I was so lonely and those years living in the city were so long, but I never lost my determination to do something with my life to support my kids.

I enrolled in an office administration course at a local college and hustled hard to balance motherhood with my studies. I didn't have money to keep a car so for over a year, I would drop my kids off at daycare and then ride a city transit bus to downtown Edmonton to study and then ride back home at the end of the day. Sometimes I would take a taxi to get my groceries, or my dad would make a trip to the city to drive me.

I moved back to Stony Plain the summer of 2003, and finished up my courses at a school there, finally earning my legal assistant diploma. It had been such a sacrifice — too bad I ended up hating that line of work. But it didn't matter. I was earning enough money to feed my kids *and* I had finally learned to type!

A few months later, I found out I was pregnant. This time it was with a guy I grew up with and knew from school. We'd slept together casually a few times and, voila, I was knocked up again and expecting my third child at twenty-three. He didn't want anything to do with me when he learned I was pregnant, but I was used to that.

I had a job at a lawyer's office in Edmonton and worked right up until giving birth to my daughter Dani in June 2004. I only took a few months off, then went back to work part-time at the lawyer's office. I also worked part-time as a waitress in the evenings. Subsidized daycare and Mom's place on the weekend were essential in helping me work and raise my three kids alone.

I loved my children with every ounce of my being. Even though I felt like the world rejected me because I was an unmarried single mother of three kids from three different (and absent) fathers, my kids were everything to me. I didn't have much to draw from when it came to good parenting skills, but I did my best and worked hard for them. I was focused.

Then Travis came along and everything changed again.

Dani was eight months old and I was twenty-four when my best friend set me up with Travis. He was five years older than me, handsome, a country boy like my dad. He was also the town drunk like my dad. I'd noticed him a few times before during his visits to the local bar. My eye always caught the one who was staggering around the most. When I found out my friend knew him, I asked for an introduction.

Our relationship started off like a hurricane that flung me right back into the partying lifestyle — subjecting my young children to parties, hangovers, and mood swings for months on end. But there was just something about Travis. I was so desperate for his affection that I became somewhat like him. I wanted to get lost in him, but I only ended up lost.

When Travis left for a three-month binge with another woman, I was distraught to the point of almost losing my mind. I didn't understand why I wasn't good enough for him to stay. I had opened my soul up to him and he left me. My vulnerable heart was smashed to pieces. My anger was back and my kids got the brunt of it. I was tired of striving, tired of trying, and told myself that if Travis couldn't love me then surely no one else could. Once again, I was burning down everything I'd built at the altar of a broken alcoholic man.

Travis had convinced me to move into a bigger place with him. When he left, I was saddled with rent I couldn't afford. No matter how hard I worked, or how many jobs I added to my already full days, I couldn't keep afloat financially. I ended up moving into another place that had a basement apartment where my dad could live so he could help pay the bills. Every step felt like I was falling backwards, but I wasn't done with my downward spiral yet.

One day, stressed, exhausted, and nearly out of my mind, I drove my kids — ages five, four, and one — over to my mom's place and unloaded them there. I told them I needed a break and I didn't know when I was coming back. And then I left. I knew in my heart that I was coming back, but I was blinded by my desperation to get away and I couldn't see anything else outside of that. I suppose it was a misguided plea for help. But it backfired big time because I sure didn't get the help I was looking for.

I went to stay with friend who lived a couple hours away in an attempt to clear my head and process the devastating blow of Travis leaving. I called my mom the next day and told her that I didn't know what I was doing or when I was coming back. She threatened to phone child welfare, but I didn't take her seriously.

When I returned two days later, my mom asked me to meet with her and some social workers at the local child services offices. I was furious that my mom had involved child services again. I didn't want their "help," I had had enough of their help to last a lifetime. But I'd lost control of the situation with my reckless actions and now I was back on their turf, only I wasn't the child in danger. It was my own children.

I remember the scene as if it were playing in slow motion. I entered a small room with a couple of couches. My mom was there along with Dani's father, Darren, Darren's mother, and a couple of social workers. It looked like an intervention. I was asked to take a seat, and I did — as far away from everyone else as possible.

I recognized one of the social workers. He'd worked at one of the group homes I'd been placed in as a kid. Memories of growing up in the system flooded back and I was filled with resentment and defiance. He leaned forward and said they wanted to "work" with me and my kids. I refused immediately.

"Well, then," he replied, his tone matter-of-fact, "we are taking your kids away from you and you can't see them for a while."

A blood-curdling noise erupted from the centre of my being. The sound that filled the room was more animal than human. It was primal. It was ancient. It was a noise that I'd never heard before and have never heard since. Tears soaked my face like a flash flood and I ran outside, choking on heavy sobs. It hit me. I was losing my children. Like my kohkum did. Like my mother did. I had failed to break the cycle.

I lost custody of my children immediately and all my rights and power as a parent were stripped from me. In many ways I was lucky that my family was there to take my children so they didn't end up with strangers. But small comfort in the midst of your greatest nightmare is not much comfort at all. They placed Faith with my sister and Luke with my mom. Dani went with her dad and his parents. I could not have contact for at least two weeks and had to follow several steps before child services would deem me fit to see them again.

I was overwhelmed with distress, fury, and no small amount of self-pity. Rather than comply with child services, I turned on them all. And I turned on myself. I didn't just start partying again, I doubled down on my self-destruction by adding drugs to the mix. Apart from the rare joint, I'd never done drugs. In truth, they scared me. But I started hanging with a crowd that snorted cocaine and one night, after a couple of drinks, I was ready to join them. I liked it. I felt on top of the world, confident and carefree. This was the escape I'd been looking for.

For about three weeks, I snorted coke every couple of days. I knew I was trudging down a dangerous path. I wasn't taking steps to see my kids but the drug was doing its job of keeping the anguish of missing them at bay. I wanted to stay in that easy carefree place instead of waking up and facing the impossible mess I had made of everything.

That all changed one night when I nearly overdosed.

It was a night when I should have been taking care of Luke. The two weeks of no contact at all had passed and I could have occasional supervised visits. Since Dad was living with me — in his basement apartment — Mom had agreed to let Luke stay the night. When both Luke and my dad were sleeping, I snuck out of the house.

I went to an acquaintance's house who was dealing drugs and started snorting lines with him. He was a hard-core user with a strong tolerance. That night he had pure, uncut white powder and he was doing a lot. He offered me line after line and it was hard to keep up with him. But I did. After a few back-to-back rounds,

I could feel that something was wrong. My heart was racing and my veins were popping out of my arms.

I panicked and got outta there in a hurry. On the blurred drive home, I gripped the steering wheel and prayed to get home safely. Miraculously, I did. It was around five in the morning and my dad's truck was gone. He had already left to go work not realizing I wasn't home. Luke was in there alone. I raced, high and horrified, to my five-year-old son's bedside. He was sleeping peacefully. The relief was palpable but didn't last long. I still had the drugs overriding my system to deal with. I kissed him shakily and went to my room.

For some reason, I sat in my bedroom closet in the dark to ride it out. It was awful. I knew I was overdosing. I could feel that I was on the verge of a heart attack. Just a week ago, an old high school friend of mine lost his girlfriend when she OD'd on cocaine at his house. She was maybe twenty years old. I got on my knees and prayed hard. I begged God to get me through and promised never to touch the drug again. The next few hours coming down were long and tormenting. But I survived.

That was the incident that finally shook me up enough to clean myself up and get my kids back. It took about a year, but I did all the programming and counselling, and followed the rules laid out by the social workers. It was the happiest day of my life when my children came back to live with me.

That doesn't mean I was a role-model mother for the rest of my days. I wish. Sometimes I'd sleep all day because I was in a deep depression. I was impatient. I yelled. I cursed. I even hit my kids a few times. And I hated myself for it, because the last thing I wanted to do was put my kids through what my parents had put us through and their parents had put them through.

I shed a lot of tears and said a lot of prayers for help to be a better mom. I made mistakes, yes. But I also told them that I loved them. I helped them when they hurt. And I fessed up when I was in the wrong. This was a new pattern and it led to a remarkable communication and openness between me and my children that I did not experience as a child with my parents. To this day, my children and I are close, resilient, and fiercely loyal to each other.

OTHER PATTERNS TOOK EVEN longer to break. Not long afterwards I got back together with Travis. He'd quit drugs and promised to get his life together for me. Our relationship was on and off, tumultuous and dysfunctional for ten years. He did give up crack, but he still drank heavily. I felt like my mom all over. I was in love with a man who was gentle like my dad, hard-working, funny, and caring. I was also chasing him around, finding him with other women, enduring endless party benders, broken promises, and the insanity of repeating the same dance over and over. But I never again allowed Travis's behaviour to be the impetus behind my own destruction.

I held on to things that inspired me, like reading. I was always an avid consumer of the written word. To me, having books around was like being surrounded by your favourite candy, except it wasn't bad for you. I also kept persuing passions that mattered to me, like writing. I kept up my writing, filling diaries and writing song lyrics. You'd find scraps of paper with scribbled ideas, poems, and stories in almost every corner of my home, just like Kohkum. Here was a pattern I didn't mind inheriting.

But the deepest, darkest pattern of all was not finished with me yet. No matter how much I grew and changed, that festering open wound of rape and the trauma of my childhood kept roiling and bubbling down in the depths. But I kept on trying to build a life on this volatile foundation. I did everything in my power to try to ignore the building pressure within.

Halfway through my twenty-ninth year I suddenly

started having vivid flashbacks from my childhood that, in turn, triggered debilitating panic attacks. I never knew when this was going to happen so my life was hijacked with the near constant feelings of terrified anticipation. Doctors drugged me with sleeping pills and other medications that made me groggy and still terrified. I knew that I needed to address the core issue, but there was no one I trusted enough to talk to.

And then it erupted.

I had a complete mental breakdown and landed on the psych ward at a hospital in Edmonton. I was diagnosed with bipolar disorder. Receiving that label was a struggle. I swallowed their pharmaceuticals and followed the advice of the doctors because I was determined to get well enough to be released from the hospital. But I was convinced that this episode was actually triggered by past traumas, not mental illness, but they did not have the right eyes to see my wounds or the right medicine to treat them.

I often sought the comfort of a bath. Lying low in the water, I could get away from the noise and the chaos of the locked-down psych ward. The water lent a lightness to my body that allowed me some relief from the heaviness of the hurting and broken souls crying from their rooms where they were caged in like animals.

One evening, I remember lying in the bath, my ears filled with the quiet swooshing of the water. My hair flowed around my naked body. I prayed to God for liberation and guidance from this lost place.

Then my eyes fluttered with lightning. In the distance I could see the farm where I grew up. I could also see the land all around it for miles, but it was cold, dark, and barren.

I heard the rattling of bones. Skeletons began rising from graves all around the farm. The beating of drums, rattles, and songs echoed in my ears. They grew louder as the skeletons rose up and began dancing. As they danced, their bones took on flesh and then the flesh took on clothes. The dancers came to life and wore beautiful, colourful regalia of feathers, hides, and beads. The land came alive alongside them, turning green and fertile. They danced and they sang as they moved out onto the lands. It felt as if they were calling to me. I didn't know them but I felt their songs pulsing powerfully through my blood as if these ancient songs were a part of me.

Then I felt myself rising out of the water with grace and strength. I was clothed in a glittering white regalia dress made of deer hide and adorned with fringes and intricate beading the likes of which I'd never seen before or since. My hair was braided in two braids and a white deer-hide headband like a crown rested on top of my head. I gasped for air as I rose up as if it was the first breath of air I had ever taken. It felt powerful, but what did it mean?

- 7 -

AFTER I WAS RELEASED from the hospital, I moved into a small two-bedroom basement apartment. Faith, Dani, and I shared one room, and Luke had the other. It was a dark and dingy place, which matched my outlook perfectly. I fell into a deep depression and most days I was barely able to crawl out of bed long enough to get the kids to school or make supper when they returned home.

This went on for a few months before I finally admitted I couldn't do it on my own and moved back in with my dad. Besides, his house had five bedrooms. That was more than enough room for us and I was paying less rent than for that crappy apartment.

It took time, but slowly I began inching my way out of that cave of depression. I prayed for guidance. I knew

I needed to find that thread of hope for a better future that had always led me out of my darkest places. My pastor recommended that I read *Unleash Your Purpose* by Dr. Myles Munroe. I hungrily devoured Munroe's message that every human being is created to fulfill a God-given destiny and if we don't share the gifts we've been given, we'll spend our lives perpetually dissatisfied. His words resonated deeply, as did his challenge for everyone to step into their heart callings. It may be risky and uncertain, but it's worth the effort of finding out.

This book reignited my desire to find my God-given purpose in life. I asked myself, after everything I'd come through, and with the wisdom I had gathered along the way, and the strength I possessed as a result: What was the calling of my heart?

The answer was easy: Writing. Not just any writing, but the kind that makes people's stories come to life. But I didn't know how or where to start again. It had been almost ten years since my brief time working at the *Red River Valley Echo*.

Then, out of nowhere a curious thought came to mind, and it startled me. *Put together a portfolio of some of your work, with a cover letter and resumé and take it to the editor at the* Spruce Grove Examiner/Stony Plain Reporter.

No way, was my immediate response. You see, at

the time, the idea of working for the newspapers of my home community meant I was shooting way too high. They were a big deal to me! With a distribution of fifty thousand and exposure to people I went to school with—who saw me as the down-and-out single mother who'd wasted her life—well, that would be my dream job. I'd be able to work in a field I was passionate about, provide a steady income for my family, *and* prove the naysayers wrong.

My negative inner soundtrack kicked in right away. *I'm not good enough. I don't have what it takes. They would never hire someone like me.* The devil's broken records of doubts played on and on.

Then again, I countered, *what if it was God encouraging me to go for it?* I had nothing to lose, really, except maybe a bit of pride from the possibility of their rejection.

I sat on the idea for a week. But I kind of knew I was going to go for it, because I was convinced that God had brought me the idea in the first place.

A WORD ABOUT MY relationship with God.

My faith in my beloved Creator and His irrevocable love for me has been a mainstay since I was a little girl. My first encounter with God was when I was five, after Mom became a Pentecostal Christian. My aunt introduced her to a charismatic church in Spruce Grove and there Mom found purpose, community, and Holy Spirit fire.

For about five years, Mom was a committed Christian who prayed in tongues, participated in healing meetings, Bible studies, worship sessions, and exuberantly shouted her "amens" during the end-of-times sermons that thundered from the pulpit every Sunday morning. Back then, I was terrified of Armageddon and the idea of Jesus returning in the near future to snatch believers back to heaven like a thief in the night. I'd kneel by my bed every evening begging Jesus not to come back yet because I still wanted to live on Earth for a while. Then I'd jump under my covers and shiver in fear, worrying that this might be the night Jesus came back with a vengeance.

Over the years in Sunday school I learned about the undying, pure, and holy love of Jesus, who wanted to live in my heart forever. As an attention-starved kid, I wholeheartedly accepted the invitation to make Jesus my saviour. And it was a decision I never regretted.

All throughout my turbulent childhood, bouncing from home to home, family to family, He was the only one who never left. He was with me through every test, every pain, every screw-up and every success. My spirit clung to Him through the years of walking through my hell on earth.

Later on, I learned about the horrors of the residential school system and what men and women "of God" did to my ancestors. Was it a struggle? Absolutely. How could such evil like the kidnapping, beating, molesting, and murdering of children because of the colour of their skin be committed under the guise of religion? The bones of thousands of Indigenous children cry out from unmarked and forgotten graves across the country, their lives taken in the name of a God who calls us to love one another. I wept and wrestled over this before I found peace in what I know to be true. Many evils have been done in the name of power, in every age and in every society. Twisting and perverting love is not a reflection of love, it is simply a reflection on those who defile it. The systems and people that committed those evils do not represent the God I know. They tried to wrest power from God for their own agenda—one so monstrous it could have been orchestrated in the pits of hell itself. But my Creator is not about death and punishment. He is about life, healing, and restoration, and I have experienced this over and over again.

Throughout my life, there have been countless times I wanted to die, but I never gave up because I felt God with me. He was there on the lonely nights I'd cry myself to sleep. He was my partner in times of dreaming up plans to one day change the world, my strength as I strove to make it happen, and my comfort when I fell on my face. And He was the strength for me to get back up again, find my feet and faith again, and keep working to give my children a better life and leave a legacy in this world to last for generations.

BACK TO THE NUDGE from God and my decision to try for a job at the paper. I decided to go for it. After all, with God backing me, I had a chance, even if the idea seemed preposterous.

I printed out a few articles I'd written (in colour to make them eye-catching), wrote a convincing cover letter, stapled my resumé to the back, and purchased a fancy folder to hold everything.

That day, after the kids left for school, I curled my hair, dolled up my face, and put on my favourite black dress that came just to my knees. I pulled it all together with burgundy knee-high suede cowboy boots with a bit of bling. I was gonna go in like a storm and make an impression!

Believe me, though, I was shaking in those boots all

the way there. I stood outside the building, took a deep breath, and said a quick prayer for courage.

A few minutes later I was sitting in a meeting room with the editor, Carson Mills. I presented my work portfolio and rambled on about my passion for writing. He thumbed through my articles and listened politely, but it was impossible to know how it was going.

"So are there any reporting jobs available here?" I finished. Less subtle than I was hoping, but certainly clear enough.

"Well," he answered, his hand stroking his chin as if in thought. "Your timing happens to be impeccable because we have an opening for a full-time staff writer."

My heart jumped, but I kept my cool. This job was for me, I just knew it. But it wasn't handed to me, I still had to work for it. I had to formally apply for the position just like everyone else, which made me nervous because I'd be up against other applicants with journalism degrees and more experience. They were hiring in two weeks and Carson generously offered me a chance to prove myself by writing a few freelance pieces before they made their decision.

I was working as a waitress at the time, so I used every spare moment in between shifts at the restaurant and Mom duties at home to get those features done.

Two weeks later I was the new staff reporter. I was going into a sink-or-swim, learn-as-you-go environment and I was expected to hit the ground running. I was ecstatic. And nervous. I was assigned a beat to cover the happenings of Parkland County. The first few times I attended council meetings I felt out of my element listening to the debates full of administrative and political jargon. I took notes ferociously and somehow pieced them together well enough to make a story out of them. It felt like I had such an important job. When I'd conduct one-on-one interviews with the mayor, I felt like I was meeting with royalty.

It is funny to look back on now because I've since questioned Canadian prime minister Justin Trudeau more than once. I've also interviewed premiers, ministerial leaders, Chiefs, powerful executives, and celebrities, but there is nothing quite like the first thrill of journalism. I loved going out to community events wearing my press pass. It was my badge of prestige. I even had business cards with my name on them: *Brandi Morin, Staff Writer, Stony Plain Reporter/Spruce Grove Examiner*. I must've held and stared at those cards for a couple hours when I first got them. Here was concrete proof that I was a professional, a real reporter determined to make my mark. I was thankful and proud.

My assignments began to include other stories in the community. I made sure to treat everyone I met with honour and interest. Even if it was just a story about a grandma making a cherry pie or a child's school project, I wanted to make their stories shine.

Carson and the other editorial staff nourished my rookie enthusiasm. My overall demeanour and outlook shifted. It was like a cloud of misfortune had parted and golden hope finally beamed into my life and my children's lives.

After a few months at the paper, I really started noticing the negative coverage of Indigenous Peoples in mainstream media. The coverage was nothing but gangs, violence, despondency, discrimination, and racism. It upset me and something tugged at my spirit to do something about it.

At the time I wasn't very connected to my Indigenous heritage. Kohkum had passed away a couple years prior and since then I'd had a hunger to learn more about my roots. I'd made some headway into learning about her background, and I was certainly aware of Parkland County's long history of colonization, broken promises, ignorance, racism, and division (like in the rest of North America), but I wanted to dig deeper. This seemed like the ideal time to take the next step.

I approached Carson with a bold idea to start a weekly feature on Indigenous perspectives. It would be called Aboriginal Aspects and I would have full creative control. The vision was to challenge the status quo on traditional media representation of Indigenous issues by cultivating relationships with First Nations and other Indigenous community members so they could speak for themselves. At the heart of the project was the concept of reconciliation and bridge building.

Carson was all for it, and I was relieved to have his backing. Aboriginal Aspects was well received in the community. Other than a few racists' phone calls to the office to cancel a subscription, most people expressed that they looked forward to learning more about their neighbours.

I travelled to nearby reserves such as the Enoch Cree Nation, Alexis Nakota Sioux First Nation, and the Paul First Nation, and met with the Chiefs and council leaders. I began to learn cultural protocol like gifting tobacco. They welcomed me, at first cautiously, but once they determined that my motives were authentic, they began to trust me with their stories. Plus, I'm Indigenous, so that helped. The more I connected, the more a fire of passion grew in me to share the depth and the profound depth of Indigenous truth. I felt like I saw my Kohkum out of the corner of my eye everywhere I went on the reserves.

I was finally home. And I was finally finding my own voice as a writer.

A colleague who was a seasoned journalist edited one of my Aboriginal Aspects features about Cree model and actress Ashley Callingbull from Enoch Cree Nation, about her courageous account of overcoming adversity. He looked up from his desk across the room after reading it and said, "This is really good. If you keep writing stuff like this, you're gonna go far."

About eight months into the job, Carson announced that he was leaving for a full-time position at the county. I was upset by the news. Carson was my biggest supporter and my own future at the paper suddenly felt a bit uncertain.

I ended up having to take a few weeks off due to a back injury in November and December of 2012. During that time, Idle No More, a grassroots movement of Indigenous sovereignty and rights, erupted across the country, partly in response to a series of omnibus bills being pushed through Canadian parliament that constituted a direct attack on First Nations sovereignty and environmental sustainability. Protection was being removed for forests and waterways on unceded and

Treaty First Nations' land as the government cleared the way for natural resources and extraction industries to operate without legal consent or environmental accountability to the Indigenous Peoples who held the rights to this land.

This was the spark that created Idle No More, but it was the generational and ongoing dismantling of environmental protection laws and the violation of human rights affecting Indigenous Peoples that stoked the flames of this movement until it burned like a wildfire across the country. There were demonstrations and protests in every major city, flash mob round dances at shopping malls, and drummers, dancers, and traditional singers were showcased to the mainstream. I watched an online news feed that followed the six-week hunger strike of Theresa Spence, a Chief from Attawapiskat. She camped in a teepee across from Parliament Hill to entice Canada's Governor General to attend a meeting with First Nations leaders to address inequality.

Witnessing the unity of Indigenous tribes and the activation of allies was unprecedented and inspiring. Yet I was frustrated by the news coverage. Reporters repeatedly got it wrong when it came to providing cultural and historical context, they perpetuated harmful stereotypes, not to mention that sometimes the news reporters themselves were downright racist in their comments. I also found it frustrating that this was the moment I was off work. I knew my small paper would not have sent me to the larger events, but still, I grieved for the lost opportunity to bring more Indigenous voices and stories to the forefront, accurately and honestly, during the brief moment when the world was listening.

I participated where I could. Shortly before I returned to work at the paper, I helped to organize an Idle No More event — a peaceful, short shutdown of a highway in Spruce Grove. About seventy-five people participated. We prayed holding hands in a circle while drummers sang a traditional song. I felt Kohkum's spirit strong around me with an intensity that I'd never experienced before. The more I reconnected with my Indigenous culture, the more I felt something powerful awakening within. It was almost like a reunion — ancient, rich, and beautiful — and I couldn't get enough.

There was much injustice to be uncovered and I recognized that as a journalist I could play a vital role in this. I couldn't wait to get back to work. But when I returned in January 2013, I felt a change in the atmosphere right away. It wasn't for the better. There was a new editor, a new reporter, and a new publisher. I braced myself for change, but when they shut down my prized Aboriginal Aspects feature I didn't see it coming. They told me something like "it has run its course."

I was devastated; to me the feature was just getting off the ground. I was confused. The world was starting to get interested in Indigenous stories and they were finally making headlines, but now was the exact moment my paper felt they were no longer relevant? I tried to fight for my feature, but they had their minds made up. A couple of weeks later my new publisher called me into her office to inform me that my feature wasn't the only thing getting the chop. I was too. I sat in front of her, stunned, as unbidden tears sprang to my eyes and her face went blurry. But I could still hear her clearly as she informed me with an air of indifference that they were "looking for different things." I packed up my desk and left in a haze.

I was back at square one. Confusion, shame, sadness, and anger dominated my emotions for the next few days. I was so sure I'd been on the right path—the one Kohkum had called me to walk and that God had opened up in front of me. Indigenous issues were having a renaissance and I had just got locked out of all of it. I just wanted to shut out the world, lie in bed, and cry. What was my purpose now?

I slipped into a bit of depression for a few months before climbing back on my feet. If I couldn't work full-time for a paper, I could still freelance and cover the stories I was passionate about. That's just what I did while landing a job as the scheduling assistant to the Alberta Leader of the Official Opposition, Danielle Smith. I was as green as new grass when it came to politics, but I admired leaders like Danielle and was fascinated by her work.

Every day I dressed the part in a blazer and heels and drove to the city to sit at my desk in a building on the legislature grounds. I felt important again, and from what I could see from afar, Danielle was the Wonder Woman of her field. She was strong, articulate, whip smart, and gorgeous. All while maintaining that "girl next door" demeanour.

The veil of admiration quickly fell off. Political affairs weren't all they were cracked up to be. I witnessed a dog-eat-dog world of dishonesty, corruption, and backstabbing. I left that job after eight months because officials began policing my freelance work. Turned out that I wasn't allowed to write about environmental and Indigenous issues after hours, even though I was just an administrative staffer. After that I was turned off politics, but in retrospect it provided me with political insight and know-how that came in handy later in my journalism career.

I was searching for my next step. I needed full-time employment and to that end, I felt a bit lost. But I continued to pour my energy into freelance writing. I had a gig I liked with *Alberta Native News* and I'd even managed to sell a piece to the Aboriginal Peoples Television Network (APTN), the world's first Indigenous television station, which was a bit of a dream of mine. None of it paid much, but if I could just keep writing on the subjects of my passion, I knew it would keep my inspiration afloat until I found my next small step on the path.

Inspiration arrived via YouTube one day in fall 2014. I had no idea when I clicked to play a video of a home-less Indigenous man that was currently going viral that I was about to find my next small step — only it was more like one giant leap.

- 8 -

"I'LL PLAY YOU TWO of them," the man says, seated in front of a red piano. He gives his nose a quick scratch. "The first one is called 'The Beginning.'"

"Okay," a woman off-camera responds.

He hesitates for just a moment, teetering slightly, and then raises his hands and hovers over the keys. A truck roars in the background.

He isn't your typical tux-and-tails pianist. He is an Indigenous man — his black hair shaggy and facial hair grown out in patches. His coat is ripped and worn, his fingernails are cracked and dirty. One can tell at a glance that he's been living rough.

And then he begins to play.

The melody is at once haunting and hopeful. Each note building on the next, weaving a story that transcends words. Despite the poor tuning, despite the one stuck key, despite the fact that the piano looks like it has had as many hard days as its player — the song rises triumphant.

The man transforms as he plays. Teetering no longer, he sways to the rhythm of the music that moves through him. He occasionally glances up at the camera, a look of profound peace on his face. As the song reaches the end, he breaks off his playing to tell the woman filming him, "I actually wrote this song." The pride is evident on his face as is the satisfaction of finally being heard. The video ends abruptly with the woman's appreciative exclamation. We never do get to hear his second song.

I don't know how long I sat in stunned silence after the video finished playing. The melody of his song "The Beginning" lingered in my body — echoing in my chest and whispering through my veins. *Listen, listen, listen*, it seemed to sing.

I clicked to play it again.

Then again.

Suddenly I knew what I had to do. I needed to find this "Piano Man" and unravel his story.

I decided to aim high and pitch my idea to the APTN *National News*. Most of their reporting is done by Indigenous journalists. I figured this story would be perfect for them. They said yes. This was my big chance, I could just feel it. Now all I had to do was find the mysterious composer. A bit of research had provided me with the basics: his name was Ryan, he was living on the streets of Edmonton, and he was gifted with a magical melody that touched the souls of millions who heard him play. It wasn't much to go on but it was a start. Edmonton was less than an hour away, so I hit the road to begin the search.

Questions raced through my mind as I drove. *What was his story? When did he discover his God-given gift? How did he feel now that he'd been "discovered"?*

The first day I went to the local homeless shelters and drop-in centres looking for Ryan. I talked with people on the streets, I drove the back streets of Edmonton and walked the alleys praying for a lead. But nothing.

The next day was the same.

The third day was a chilly Saturday in early November. Since it was the weekend, I took my daughter Dani with me. She was ten at the time and liked to join me on assignments whenever possible and appropriate. I'd told her all about the extraordinary man we were searching for and she'd watched the video with the same fascination as I had.

We walked the streets and made the rounds as I'd

done the two previous days — still nothing. Then I got a tip from someone on the street to check out the Catholic cathedral downtown. Ryan liked to panhandle there and sometimes played the grand piano inside the church.

The cathedral was located in a rough part of town, known for its population of panhandlers, addicts, and downtrodden people. Ryan wasn't outside the church, so Dani and I headed inside to check it out. We sucked in our breath when we stepped through the doors. The exquisite architecture along with the fifty-foot stained-glass windows depicting the dramatic life and death of Jesus created an atmosphere that was both stunning and serene. The marble floor and cedar pews gleamed in the low light. It was a haven tucked among the boulevards of hell.

The church was empty, and the silence amplified the awe and wonder Dani and I felt in that magnificent place. We decided to take a moment to pray. I heard Dani's little voice praying that we would find Ryan soon so Mom could share his inspiring story with the world. "Amen," I murmured, and then we headed outside once more.

It was afternoon by then and I decided to make another round driving the downtown area. My route was aimless as Dani and I scanned crowds for Ryan's face. We were on Jasper Avenue waiting to turn left at a set of lights. To my right, I noticed a crowd crossing the street and I turned to check them out. They were walking next to the Fairmont Hotel Macdonald. My eyes cut to that nightmare building next door where I'd been held captive as a child. It towered like a menacing shadow. My head spun and I gripped the steering wheel to steady myself.

And then I was distracted again. In that crowd, a familiar face gleamed like a ray of redemption—Ryan! I wasn't taking any chances of losing him. I put my car in park, right there in the left-hand turning lane, and leapt out, yelling his name across the road and frantically waving him over. Ryan looked my way and then started walking towards us. Dani kept an eye on Ryan approaching and I got back in my car and pulled over to park.

His thick black hair from the video had been shaved to a shadow of stubble. The tongues of his sneakers were hanging out and the laces were missing. He wore a white hospital band on his wrist and was taking swigs of Listerine out of a plastic bag. I introduced myself as a journalist and asked if I could spend some time with him for a story. With a near toothless smile of curiosity, he explained he didn't have any plans and agreed to hang out for the rest of the day.

I hated seeing him sipping Listerine, so I bought

him a six-pack of beer. Then we went to an outdoor park and made ourselves comfortable on a bench. Dani observed quietly and with great interest as I took a couple of pictures and videos with my camera and then set my phone to record. I asked him how he felt about his sudden fame from the viral video and the widespread recognition of his talent.

"I've waited over twenty years for this," Ryan told me with a gummy grin. "Last year I went into the Macdonald Hotel and asked if they minded if I played one of their grand pianos . . . " My throat temporarily closed at the mention of that hotel but I forced myself to stay focused on his story. "Security escorted me there. I played Beethoven. They were in tears."

As Ryan continued to share, more and more similarities between us emerged. I felt as if my own song was playing in the background, quietly adding notes of harmony to Ryan's ballad. He too grew up in foster homes, telling me they were "the only thing" he knew. At thirteen he ran away and made his home on the streets. He said he wouldn't have it any other way. He was more at home on the streets than in any building or authority that threatened to contain him. I felt a deep sadness that such a talented person had lived such a limited life, but Ryan asserted that he was a happy person.

"I'm never grumpy or angry," he said while taking a swig of beer, "because anger, it affects the music, you almost forget how to play."

He was eager to share his playing with Dani and me, so I suggested that we head to the Royal Alexandra Hospital which I knew kept a piano in the lobby. It also happened to be where I was born. When he sat to play at the piano, he transformed. He was no longer a homeless alcoholic, no longer a person everyone looked through or crossed the street to avoid. He was music. He was hope. This was his voice. And a crowd gathered to listen.

After he was finished, I took him to a restaurant for lunch. Between mouthfuls, he told us more stories, which Dani gobbled up. Some of the things he shared were very difficult and I knew it would be hard for my daughter to hear them. But it was important for her to understand that there were people in the world who suffered, who lived this way, and she should know that truth. Afterwards, it was time for us to head home. Ryan asked to be dropped off at the St. Joseph's Basilica where he could play before they locked their doors for the night. Just outside, I offered him my phone to call his mother to tell her the news about his new-found success. He told me it'd been years since he'd talked to her. Their relationship was deeply troubled as she'd been unable to care for her kids due to struggling with trauma and addictions of her own.

"Have you heard the news, Mom?" he shouted down the line with excitement when she picked up. "I made it. I made it, Mom." I could hear her crying on the other end. Dani's small hand was warm in mine.

It was hard to leave him there and drive away. His life was so precarious. He had fame, but was he safe? Would it make any difference? Would he live to keep sharing his story and gift of music with the world or would he be forgotten? With tears and a lump in my throat I drove home. But I was also fuelled by a steely determination. It was my turn to apply my gifts to make sure Ryan's story rippled out even further.

I wrote the story up for APTN, submitted it, and eagerly anticipated the roaring response of approval from my editor. But when he called, it wasn't what I expected. Instead of praise, I was on the receiving end of a pep talk. They wanted a rewrite.

"Brandi, I know you have this in you," said Kenneth Jackson. "Describe him, make him come alive with your words. Let's show Ryan to the world in a powerful way."

I was instantly flooded with shame and a feeling of

inadequacy. Why did I think I was good enough for the APTN? But Kenneth hadn't rejected my piece outright. I would just have to find my courage and try again.

I breathed in deeply. *I'm going to do this. I'm going to blow them out of the water with this story.* Then I prayed. And then I wrote. I opened a blank page and channelled all the emotions I had experienced while meeting Ryan. I felt the pretenses and pressures drop away. I heard my own song playing in the background as the words burned a path along the page.

ABOUT TWO WEEKS LATER, I got a call from the news director at APTN. They loved my piece and wanted to offer me a paid two-week, fast-track training for video journalism. The only catch was, I had to get to Winnipeg — 1,400 kilometres away. And I had to get there in two weeks.

I wasn't about to let this opportunity slip by. Frantically, I arranged child care for my kids, got an oil change in my fifteen-year-old beat-up red Pontiac, and hit the road.

The training was intense. I was juggling the demanding pace of learning with an equally demanding home life that I was managing from a distance. I so badly wanted to be a storyteller so I could keep on moving up in my career.

At the end of the training, APTN offered me a four-month internship in Winnipeg that would start in three weeks. I worried about the impact on my kids. This was my dream, yes, but I was no longer willing to chase something if it meant I couldn't be the mom they needed. Besides, I didn't even know what would come of it. It was an internship with no guarantees on the other side. But my kids were older and I had to remind myself that this was not the same as leaving them when they were young. I could say yes to this opportunity and also be a responsible mother. In fact, I knew that part of being a responsible mother was modelling a life of taking risks for our dreams. It was decided.

Faith and Luke stayed with my mom and Dani stayed with her dad. We all agreed to keep in touch over FaceTime. "Before you know it," I promised them, "I'll be back." They all wished me luck.

Despite my steady reassurances to my kids, I was scared packing up and going alone. But I had faith that this was meant to be. Once again, I felt that I was on the path that God had prepared for me.

Not long into my internship my news director, Karyn Pugliese, came up to my desk and asked if I could do a live hit for the news team in Ottawa. A few things about Karyn: she's tiny in stature, soft in demeanour, but thunderously fervent in all she does. I'd been awed and a little intimidated by her since beginning my internship, but also thrilled at the chance to learn from this powerhouse of a journalist and visionary leader.

"Of course I'll do the live hit," I answered enthusiastically.

"Great, it's in fifteen minutes, get ready," she said.

I almost fainted when she walked away. I ran to the bathroom to fix my makeup and fluff my hair. Standing there looking in the mirror and realizing that I was about to be on TV sent me into a panic. I locked myself in one of the bathroom stalls and called my long-time friend Maxine. I told her that I needed help, and asked her to pray with me. She did and assured me everything would be fine. "You're living in your purpose, Brandi. Don't forget that!" she reminded me. "God is with you and even if you're scared, you can do it."

She was right. I hung up the phone and stepped from the stall. I was still shaking but I took a breath and reached inside to the woman who is stubborn, eager, and unfaltering. I put on a smile, gave my hair a tousle, and headed to the control room.

They had a teleprompter, so I didn't need to speak

off-the-cuff (phew), but I knew I would have to read without stumbling and would have to answer any questions with unscripted material—and answer accurately. I looked into the camera and time slowed down. Then it was over. I had passed! It all went fairly well for my first time. Soon I was thrown into these kinds of scenarios all the time. My time at APTN was the best way for me to learn the ropes and was how I would come into my courage in a bigger way.

Over the next four months, as spring came to a close, I packed up my stuff from the crumbling, low-budget motel that had been my home during my time in Winnipeg and drove westward. I was heading back to Stony Plain, Alberta. Back to my little town that held my house and my kids, as well as the many memories of heartache and letdowns over the years. But I was coming back with a new dream. This was the start of big things.

I was counting down the kilometres with each roadside sign that raced by, surrounded by endless prairie fields just greening with the year's new wheat. I couldn't wait to begin my life as a national reporter for the APTN *National News*. I was becoming someone. I was making a difference. I squared my shoulders, lifted my chin, and clutched the steering wheel just a bit tighter. Everyone better get ready for me.

– 9 –

IN 2016, WHEN THE federal government announced the National Inquiry into Missing and Murdered Indigenous Women and Girls, I was thirty-six years old and had been working for APTN for over a year. Tina Fontaine's death, two years earlier, had finally galvanized the nation to stand with the family members, survivors, and grassroots activists who had been demanding a national investigation into this crisis for years.

Like any ambitious endeavour, the National Inquiry had a number of logistical and bureaucratic kinks to work out as they launched and began to figure out how they would undertake this highly complex and sensitive work. The mainstream media jumped on every misstep or staffing change with an almost malicious delight, reporting that the inquiry was mired in controversy and confusion. The criticism from mainstream society was rapid and vicious. Instead of insisting on improvements to the process, the majority of coverage focused on calling for the inquiry to be shut down altogether to "quit wasting taxpayers' money." The implication of such calls was that Indigenous women and girls were worthless. It was all so ugly and violent that I felt sick. They didn't even know what, or *who*, they were talking about. Why were they the spokespeople of this movement?

I was a member of the media. I was an Indigenous woman. And I was a survivor of rape, even though I had told almost no one about this. For the first time in my life, I felt a compulsion to share my personal story. I wanted people to see who we really are. To see that we matter. Indigenous women do not conform to the stereotype to which colonialist society tries to reduce us.

"Karyn, I want to write my story of survival," I told my news director. "It's important to speak out."

"Brandi, are you sure?" she asked. "This is very personal. I want you to be okay."

"I'm going to be fine," I assured her. I knew I was no longer that frightened child. I was strong now. "Please, I want to do this," I pushed.

She gave me the go-ahead and paired me with a colleague, Jorge Barrera, to write the piece. Jorge, a brilliant journalist (who later worked for CBC Indigenous), told me to sit down and just let the entire story out in raw form. "Don't hold anything back," he advised. "Just write, and we'll go from there."

That's what I did. I opened the door that had been locked for so long and let the monsters of memory come roaring out. Suddenly I was that child again, reliving everything—the rapes, rejections, abuse. My body felt every memory, flooded with the shame of believing I was to blame for everything. I felt fear's claws digging into my mind.

Hang on, Brandi, hang on, I told myself. *You're tough, brush this off!* I was determined that fear would not hold me prisoner any longer and that the healing of this wound—once and for all—was on the horizon. If I could just push through and write this story.

I did, and my story was published. In truth, there was no obvious impact. It seemed to be absorbed quietly into the hundreds of conversations happening around the inquiry, but I still felt good about it. I'd done my part to help give voice to our women. And I'd faced down my monsters through the power of my journalism career. I could finally move forward. Or so I thought.

. . .

ONLY A COUPLE WEEKS later, I was confronting yet another area in my life that had been bound fast by fear: I was boarding a plane. There was a big climate change meeting between Indigenous leaders and Prime Minister Trudeau taking place in Vancouver and I was going to be there to cover it. It was the first time I'd been on a plane in almost ten years. The feeling of being completely out of control, thousands of feet in the sky, and knowing your life could come crashing to the ground at any second was horrifying to me. I think I inherited the fear from my kohkum—she couldn't stand flying either. Regardless of the source, I couldn't go near an airport without triggering a debilitating panic attack.

But I knew that the fear of flying was holding me back from what I was meant to do. I had already turned down opportunities to cover stories with APTN that had required flying to a distant location. I'd always covered up my phobia with some sort of excuse for why I couldn't go. Well, I was done making excuses. This was the season of Brandi conquering her fears. It was time to break free and soar. Literally.

This didn't mean I had to do it all on my own though. I invited my close friend, Nicole Robertson, a beautiful Cree media guru and former journalist, to come with me. She held my hand when the plane took off and prayed with me during the landing when my heart felt like it'd fail. When those wheels hit the tarmac, I was still terrified but I was so friggin' proud of myself. Take *that*, fear of flying! Anything was possible now. I bought a pair of glittery golden shoes to celebrate and that night Nicole and I danced barefoot in the surf of the Pacific Ocean.

A few days later, I boarded another flight, this time to Calgary to cover a ceremony by the Tsuut'ina Nation to honour Trudeau. It was a beautiful and elaborate affair. They offered blessings and crowned Trudeau with a war bonnet. It was adorned with eagle feathers, signifying honour and respect, and he was given a Tsuut'ina name, Gumistiyi, meaning "he who keeps trying." The prime minister joined hands with hundreds of Chiefs and danced around the ballroom to the nation's beats of the sacred drums and cheers of hope. And I got to be there, my own hope blooming in my chest. My better days had finally arrived. But they weren't going to stay.

Shortly after I returned home, my mom went into the Royal Alex Hospital in Edmonton for a simple stomach surgery. But it turned deadly when a surgeon snipped her intestines, which started leaking toxins into her bloodstream. My siblings and I rushed to the hospital, and the next thing I knew, I was standing in the intensive care unit staring at the unrecognizable body of my mother. She was unconscious, her whole body was blown up and bloated, and there were countless tubes twisting and snaking in and out of her. I could hear the doctors telling us that she was septic and they didn't know if she would live, but it was like their voices were coming from a great distance. My entire focus was fixed on my mother.

I bent over her bed and spoke to her quietly. "Mom, I love you. Mom, are you okay in there?" I stroked her hand and then her face. Something began to stir in my belly. Something big. I couldn't lose my mom yet, we still had unfinished business. There was so much still to say, apologies to make, past wounds to heal. "Mom, hang on, okay? It's too soon for you to go..."

The pain hit hard and fast as something ripped open deep inside and I doubled over. I began sobbing, sucking each breath into lungs that wouldn't expand. I could feel myself beginning to fall into that dark open pit inside of me.

My youngest brother, Joel, and my older sister, Prista, helped me from the room and brought me outside. I couldn't stop sobbing and was clinging to my brother's strong arms and shoulders because my knees couldn't hold my weight. It felt surreal, like I was watching all of it from a great distance.

The next few days, I tried to push on with my life — work, kids, caring for Mom — but the open wound inside pulled at me incessantly. I felt like I was clinging to its edge by my fingertips. I was bombarded with severe panic attacks and bouts of uncontrollable crying during the day and insomnia at night. When I did snatch some sleep, I woke screaming from horrendous nightmares. The days and nights bled into each other.

I wasn't eating, I was weak, and my body trembled with grief. Millimetre by millimetre, I could feel myself slipping. And then I fell. Down, down, down. From the pinnacle of my recent triumph, I tumbled lower than I had ever gone before — right into the open maw of hell that gaped at the centre of my being. I ended up back on the psych ward — that all-too-familiar oppressive and colourless institution — once more in the grip of psychosis.

It was a horrifying experience. I saw things that weren't there and heard screaming that no one else did. Perhaps because it was coming from inside me. Over and over again, my mind was tortured by dark scenes from my childhood. For weeks I couldn't sleep if I was alone. I would beg a nurse to come with me and tuck me in and tell me everything was going to be okay. I was a child again. Alone, institutionalized, and powerless to help myself. Meanwhile my mother languished at some other hospital and I could do nothing to save her either.

My psychiatrist prescribed an arsenal of drugs—anti-psychosis, anti-anxiety, bipolar meds, and sleeping pills. I became a walking zombie. This was not the medicine I wanted, nor the medicine I believed I needed, but I complied with everything. I just wanted to be better.

OVER THE NEXT FOUR months I was in and out of hospital while my mother fought for her life in another hospital across the city. My psychosis passed and in its place a severe depression took hold, unlike anything I'd ever experienced in my life. The complete blackness of it erased any memory of how far I'd come and blotted out any light of hope for my future.

Face it, Brandi. This is you. The darkness, like smoke, drifted through my mind. *You can try and run. You can try and pretend you are someone else. But I will always get you back. You will always be a broken nothing.* The only relief from these voices came when the heavy medications dragged me into fitful sleep. Even still, from deep within that dark pit, I was still fighting. Some part of me believed I would make it out alive and well. And I was willing to do anything to get out of the abyss of despair and return to my normal life.

"BRANDI, YOU KNOW WE'VE talked about this before." My psychiatrist leaned in, and behind her trendy black-framed glasses her eyes reflected her typical compassion. Her short blond bob framed her pretty face. She spoke with a British accent that was slightly comforting — but only slightly, given the nature of our conversation. She looked at me seriously. "I think we need to start the ECT. I *know* how you feel about it but this therapy has come a long way and it's safe and effective. I really believe it's going to help you recover quickly."

She was talking about electroconvulsive therapy, also known as electroshock therapy. We'd had this conversation more than once over the years and every time I had vehemently refused. *Hello?!* We're talking about shocking your brain with electricity! That's the type of thing we see in horror movies. I didn't care what the research said, I wasn't down for electrocution.

I was so tired though. It had been seven months since that day I visited my mom's hospital room and I was tired of this endless internal battle. Tired of returning to the cold, lonely walls of the hospital. I didn't have it in me to fight anymore. I knew my mom would've vehemently argued against my getting this treatment had she been coherent. But there wasn't really anyone to counsel me. I was alone. I was desperate. I agreed.

I can remember the first treatment.

I left my room at 6:00 a.m. and walked down the corridor to the ECT unit and checked in at the desk. I sat in the dim waiting room until my name was called. I was led into a white-and-blue operating room with a bed in the centre of it. There was medical equipment everywhere, the steel surfaces gleamed and reflected the glaring overhead lights. The smell of sanitizing alcohol was strong. I climbed onto the hospital gurney as the nurses talked to me in their kind, soothing voices. They might have asked me how I was, or perhaps shared a joke while strapping down my legs and arms. Another nurse inserted an IV into my arm. The room began to fill with busy medical personnel, scurrying around as they completed the final preparation. Then the anesthesiologist was at my side, injecting the anesthetic into my IV. For a moment, I felt euphoric...

The memories that follow are less clear.

I woke up in the hallway, still strapped to the gurney, groggy but alive. They wheeled me back to my room on the ward, monitored my heart rate and blood pressure for an hour, and that was that.

I walked that corridor at six o'clock three mornings a week for three weeks, although it felt more like I was floating above my body just going through the motions. I can't tell you much more than that about those three weeks apart from the occasional flash of a memory fragment: in the waiting room; shuffling down the hallway; the numb terror that my brain might never recover from what they were doing and I would live as a zombie for the rest of my life.

Here is what I can tell you with absolute clarity: ECT did not help me. I didn't get better. There was no miraculous turnaround for me. It *did* wipe out huge pockets of my memories from earlier in the year and made me forget periods of time during the day. That was scary. After nine sessions I dropped out. I was supposed to have three more treatments but I knew it wasn't doing anything for me and I didn't want to fry my brain any longer.

I know now that the only thing accomplished during those weeks was that another layer of trauma was slathered on top of my past traumas. Once again, a failed system had offered me the wrong medicine. This was not how I was going to heal. I needed to trust myself again.

Thank God I tapped into that instinct for survival within myself that had kept me going so many times before.

Eventually, I was released from the hospital, still on a number of drugs for anxiety, bipolar disorder, and insomnia, but at least I was home. The next step was returning to my life. It was an agonizingly slow recovery for the first few months. I still had panic attacks whenever I left the house and needed company constantly.

My mother was undergoing a parallel journey of recovery. She had to learn to walk again and had multiple debilitating medical complications. She eventually made it home from the hospital as well but her struggle was far from over. She had a long journey of rehabilitation in front of her that would end up taking years. I've never seen her cry so many tears of defeat and sadness. But her spirit was strong, as was her determination to find a way through no matter what — a capacity I believe she passed on to me.

When I returned to work at APTN, five months later, in the new year, I was still afraid to travel outside of my hometown alone. The moment I ventured too far from home, my mind and body immediately reacted as if my life was in danger, reducing me to a huddling, sobbing mess. The woman in sparkly shoes who had conquered her fear of flying was nothing more than a distant memory. But I couldn't be a reporter who couldn't travel outside her small town. I had to figure this out.

My daughter Faith, who was eighteen at the time, agreed to travel with me for my first few out-of-town assignments. She loved to travel and I loved her calm and gentle spirit. It was a great solution and I was so grateful for her support. There were others who also helped during those early days of finding my way back into the world. One elder friend of mine, Yvonne Owen, was a huge support. Nighttime anxiety continued to be a problem for months, even with sleeping pills. So every night around nine o'clock, I'd call Yvonne and every night she'd pick up and I'd feel her love radiating down the phone line. She'd pray with me in her gentle, sweet voice and offer all the assurances I needed until I felt safe enough to rest.

I started counselling with Mary-Anne, a phenomenal therapist from my church. I wanted to deal with the monsters of my past decisively and that meant honouring what had always worked for me: my community and my faith. With Mary-Anne's guidance and God's steadfast support I was able to start peeling back the years of trauma and hardship, layer by painful layer. Whenever I'd grow impatient at how long it all seemed to be taking or start comparing myself to others, Mary-Anne helped me to remember that everyone is different in the ways they process trauma and approach healing, and that there is no formula — it is just a brave journey forward one step at a time.

By the spring of 2017, I was finally back on the job full-time. My world had been shaken to its very foundations, and I was out the other side with my feet planted on terra firma. I was ready to make up for lost time. I was also ready for a professional change. I'd worked as a correspondent for APTN for two years. They had given me so much to help me strengthen my skills as a journalist and to learn broadcasting. I knew I would always be grateful to have worked at the world's first and only national Indigenous broadcaster, but it was time for something new.

I worked as a freelancer over the summer while I considered my next steps. I also rekindled my relationship with Travis — the man I had been in and out of a toxic relationship with for over a decade. We had been apart for two years but I reached out to him in a moment of weakness, loneliness, and uncertainty. Some small part of me registered that just as I was taking bold steps forward in my professional life, I seemed to be regressing in my personal life, but it was not enough to stop me from heading back down this path. I was looking for the familiar, for the comfort of him to embrace me and help quell the pains of my failures and my past which still haunted me. He had gotten sober and I gave him a chance.

That summer was good for us. We hiked the Rocky Mountains and fished the numerous lakes around us. We both loved fishing. He was my date to my younger brother's wedding and my companion on those nights you just want to watch TV at home. That autumn, I found out I was pregnant. It was a huge shocker. We'd used protection and had not seen this coming. But we welcomed the news and were excited to become parents *together* for the first time. We moved in together and committed to doing whatever it would take for our coming baby to have the best shot, with healthy parents.

I didn't know what another baby meant for my career and I wondered if my life as a journalist was over. I'd come so far though, and I resolved that I could be a new mom and still have a career. I was at peace with all of it and for the first time ever, I was able to enjoy my pregnancy, lost in the wonder of it and feeling grateful.

WHEN I WAS ABOUT six months pregnant, I got news that Ryan the "Piano Man" had died. My heart sank.

I was thankful to hear that he'd been living at an inner-city housing project and not in some back alley when he passed. He was found in his apartment. It seemed he simply fell asleep on his couch and didn't wake up. He was sober. He had an electric piano in his living room and had been composing new songs. It was the peaceful end that Ryan deserved.

His family invited me to his funeral. They were bringing him home to the Alexander First Nation, west of Edmonton. I told them I would be honoured to attend. Dani went with me.

The funeral and reception were held at the community hall. The smell of traditional foods like moose stew and fresh bannock permeated the room. It was set up with long tables and chairs and dozens of mourners feasted together in Ryan's honour. I approached Ryan's open coffin to pay my respects.

Ryan was beautiful in death, even though he looked much older than his forty-six years on earth. His hair had grown out almost to his shoulders and was braided. He was dressed in a silk ribbon shirt with a beaded medallion of a red piano around his neck. Among the photos placed around the casket, I spotted a couple of him and me together.

"Ryan, I'm sorry you lived this hard life. Alone. Lost.

Outcast. Wandering," I told him, softly. "But I'm so happy. Happy you shared your gifts and music with the world. You know you're famous, right? Just like you wanted to be."

After the funeral I met his mother and his brother, Blake. He attended the funeral in chains and an orange jumpsuit, accompanied by armed guards. He had been released for only a few hours so he could say goodbye to his brother. He told me that the two of them had been homeless together. Blake was also a musician as well as an incredible singer, and the brothers would jam together while sitting on cardboard boxes in back alleys in downtown Edmonton.

I thought about Ryan a lot after the funeral. My belly was growing, my path uncertain once again, but his words kept burning in my heart. "I'm not a religious person, but I believe in the Creator and I thank the Creator for giving me this gift. If there's anybody out there — a piano player, guitar, drums, or whatever — don't be scared to come out of the shadows and play, perform." They were a constant reminder to me that life was too short to hide in the shadows. We were meant to share, to shine and create. I had a new baby and also Ryan to live for now.

. . .

THE NEXT FEW MONTHS brought miracle after miracle into my life. I got a gig with the CBC as a full-time reporter for their newly established CBC Indigenous unit. Can you imagine, little ol' me at the CBC? Even more miraculous was the birth of my beautiful daughter, Elaysia. It was so different to welcome a baby into a life that was steady and felt full of passion and purpose. I loved every minute of it and the time flew by.

After about two years I left my position at the CBC. Even though I was full of gratitude for my time there, I once again felt I had outgrown that vehicle for my work. I wanted to soar higher and farther. I wanted to reach the world by telling the Indigenous stories that *I* wanted to tell.

It was a gamble. There were no certainties for me as I closed the door on the CBC, and I did have a financial bump in the road that sent me back to living with my dad, but becoming a freelance independent journalist was the best decision I could have made. My dream for international coverage was just around the corner. Starting with the *New York Times*.

- 10 -

ABOUT SEVEN MONTHS AFTER I assisted Dan Bilefsky with the story about Tina Fontaine for the *New York Times*, I went on to work with Al Jazeera English. Another professional pinnacle reached! My career was unquestionably on the rise. I was pitching my story ideas to top international media organizations and they were biting. My platform as a journalist was allowing me to bring greater and greater attention to the systemic inequality and violence that so disproportionally targets Indigenous Peoples. I was becoming increasingly known through my work as a champion for justice and as a voice for serious, compassionate, and long-overdue reconciliation.

So there was my career, rocketing skyward beyond my wildest dreams. (Okay, well, maybe not, because I have some big dreams and they're pretty wild. Like,

I'm talking world-changer, history-maker, badass, mother-warrior stuff.) But the question that plagued me was: How could I be doing so well in my professional life but be epically failing in my personal life?

I still woke in the mornings flooded with intense fear from nightmares. I didn't understand it. My public image was that of a strong Indigenous woman and yet behind closed doors I felt like an emotional weakling.

I suppose some of my nightmares were understandable. I had just lost a son when he was born during my sixth month of pregnancy in December 2019. It was a sudden, horrendous, bloody passage from life to death. Judah died of a blood infection that he caught from me. The doctors didn't detect the infection until it was too late.

My entire family was with me. I don't think I've ever heard my mom wail like she did when he died. She was pacing the hospital room mourning so loudly for her grandchild that she could be heard all the way down the hall. Travis was Judah's father. He was on the ground in the corner, head down, nose dripping, and tears pouring from his eyes. Faith was also there, along with my sister and an elder from church—everyone was scrambling, crying. The collective grief that swelled to fill that space ached with the trauma of this horrendous loss and behind it, I could feel all of our losses that had come before.

I was in a daze. Flesh of my flesh, who had been kicking and moving in response to my hand placed on my belly just hours before: He couldn't be gone. I couldn't understand it.

I held my beautiful, tiny, one-pound baby boy for a day and a half before they took him to the funeral home. The hospital had a special bassinet for stillborn babies that helped preserve them. In between holding him, kissing him, telling him how much I missed and loved him, I would place him back into the bassinet beside me. He smelled so amazing, like roses and cinnamon. We had his funeral and buried him in a miniature white casket wrapped in a soft baby-blue blanket and white bonnet. I picked a spot in St. Albert, Alberta, down the hill from where Kohkum is buried. I wanted him to be near her so she could look out for him, until we are together again. She knew the loss of a stillborn son too, so I know he is in good hands.

I WENT BACK TO work within three weeks. This was not an avoidance tactic; this was my way of healing. I'd come to learn that telling other people's stories of pain, resilience, and resistance offered me a way to move through my own pain. Perhaps this was why my career felt stable even though my personal life did not.

In large part, I knew the problem was linked to the fact that I was still with Travis. He was a great father to Elaysia and would have been a good father to Judah too, but our relationship had long gone sour. His infidelity, secrets, and disappearances twisted my guts with insecurity and jealousy. I tried to let him go but we always found our way back to each other, and the whiplash was wearing me down.

It would go something like this: I'd finally have enough of his antics, pull together what dignity I had left, and declare it over. Then I'd end up on the phone with him cooing down the line, "Trav, it's good to hear your voice. Elaysia would love to see you and, well, I miss you too. How about we meet up...?"

That was all it took. Travis loved me in his own broken way, and I couldn't stomach the ugly, skin-crawling feeling of abandonment that consumed me whenever he was gone for too long. So we'd have a week or so of that honeymoon feeling before things went back to usual—Travis gone for days, not returning calls, and hanging around with shady people and, I imagine, doing shady things.

That's when the guilt set in. It crept over me like a stinking, weighted blanket. I was trapped, again. I also felt like a hypocrite — look at me, the strong Indigenous woman role model.

There had to be a way out. How had I gotten out of my messes before? Oh right, with prayer and support. I said a quick prayer and texted my therapist.

"Mary-Anne, can we have an emergency session, please? FaceTime? My life is falling apart."

She was free and jumped onscreen to chat with me, which is precisely when I realized the state of my physical appearance. My hair was slightly greasy and piled messily on top of my head. It was day two of the sweats and tank top with no bra. I had deep bags under my eyes. But I had long developed the kind of relationship with Mary-Anne where I was safe to show up exactly as I was. I launched right in.

"Mary-Anne, I've eaten a whole big bag of Doritos, emptied the candy jar, and can't stop looking for more to shove in my face! I've smoked at least a half pack of cigarettes today and in between I stay in bed." I looked down at my stomach and grimaced at the weight I was gaining back after working so hard to lose it for my fortieth birthday a few months before. Depression and weight. That's what I got whenever I had Travis around in my life.

"I can't face the world, Mary-Anne," I continued. "I'm a failure. Why can't I just shake this? Why can't I shake him?"

A pressure was beginning to build in my chest. I hadn't had a full-out panic attack in years and my God, I didn't need one now. My heart was beginning to thump like the hoofs of the four horsemen. It helped to hear Mary-Anne's soft, serene, and steadying voice, but what she said next shook me to my core.

"Brandi, I think this is about attachment."

Okay, she had my attention.

"Your childhood in the foster system prevented you from forming any deep and safe attachments as a child. We all need to feel attached and loved. You keep transferring this unmet need to the men in your life. That's the issue with Travis. He's the only one you're really attached to and you're terrified to lose that, even if it's a rotten thing."

I took a long breath. It felt like some sort of weight was literally falling from my shoulders. Suddenly I was connecting dots within my own life.

She was right. I was close with my parents and family. I had acquaintances, mentors, deep support systems, but there was only a minimal level of intimacy. I was still holding everyone at arm's-length. The only people I let in past my childhood walls of defence were the men I'd hope would see me for who I am and love me uncondi- tionally—finally proving that I was good enough. No wonder my relationships felt like life and death. And no wonder I had a hard time letting go.

And then the dots I was connecting stretched out farther than me, lighting up a trail across the women in my family through the generations.

I thought of my kohkum. Child of the residential school system and all the trauma of loss of identity and family that came with it. She grew up to be a single mom in a series of crappy relationships with men who didn't see her worth. They used and abused her, but she stayed with them, because she needed someone. Kohkum had also had nightmares all her life.

Then there was my parents' relationship. My rela- tionship with Travis could have been a carbon copy. The connections were so obvious. I marvelled at the pattern so clearly in front of me and that gave me hope. Relief. Now that I could see it, I could see my way out of it.

I shook my head. Here I was, all this time, looking at the macro view and calling the world's attention to the devastation of inherited trauma on Indigenous Peoples, but had failed to see the micro view of all the ways it played out in my own life.

I'd seen some of the cycles of pain in my family. I'd been working for years to break the pattern of traumatized parenthood and help my kids have a different life. But that day, everything shifted. It was like I heard a click in my mind and instead of having to battle the shackles, they simply fell away. My heart was no longer stuck on the same circular path.

AFTER MY REVELATORY CALL with Mary-Anne, I had to jump on a Zoom meeting with a grade-ten student from Ontario. She was doing a research project on missing and murdered Indigenous women and girls and came across my work online and wanted to talk to me about it. It was an interesting experience as a journalist, who is so used to interviewing others, to be the one being asked the questions. I studied her young face on the camera, filled with optimism and passion. She reminded me of myself at her age — quick and eager to take on the world and fight to right the wrongs of society. I was impressed by her vigour and the questions she had prepared. I told her she would make a great reporter one day. She beamed from the compliment.

I didn't know her life, if she had a healthy family or if she was bogged down by dysfunction and adversity like

I had been. But I felt a profound hope for her, that she might find her way to the success she desires. And I felt a profound gratitude for being one of the lights along her path. I could be that person to her, broken as I am. Once again, I recognized that our path of reconciliation, among one another, within ourselves, has never been about getting it perfect.

I'M STILL ON THE journey of recuperating from trauma. At forty-one years old, I still struggle to resolve what happened to me. But there's beauty in this. I think about how in Japanese culture, when an object of value breaks into pieces, they don't throw it away. They glue it back together with gold. The end result is an object that is more precious, valuable, and beautiful than it was before it was broken. It's called the art of Kintsugi and it reminds all of us that broken objects aren't something to hide, but to display with pride.

I feel like a woman of gold. With every wound that heals, I have a scar that flashes golden in the light. If you take the time to look at me the right way, you will see trails of fire up and down my skin, set ablaze by the rising sun. When I take the time to look at you — I see the same.

- 11 -

IN 2008, MY KOHKUM, on her deathbed, burst into Cree as she blessed her children who surrounded her. None of them knew what the words meant as they didn't speak Cree, but even hearing the story second-hand, some part of me understood the meaning beyond the words: *Listen up, we are older and more powerful than this moment. Wake up, we have been sleeping for too long. Rise up, we have been held down for too long.* My kohkum's words opened a new path before me and step by step I have been walking it ever since. I have fallen many, many times, but each time I have felt the strength and steadiness of her hands on one side of me, and God's on the other, as they helped me to rise and keep walking.

The early days of walking this path consisted largely

of getting to know Kohkum's history, which was in turn, my own.

In 2011 I started to learn about residential schools, starting with the one Kohkum attended. I always knew Kohkum went to the "convent"; that's what she called the school she attended in St. Albert after her father passed away of TB in 1944. Her mother was alone with the children and had no choice but to go and live at the Catholic residential school as a maid and enroll her kids there. Kohkum talked about it here and there during her life, but never a lot. She'd tell me about how strict the nuns were and how she couldn't talk to her brothers because the boys and girls were separated and it was a "sin" to even look at the boys. She mentioned that the uniforms they were given were annoyingly itchy but they had to sit completely still in church so she would pinch herself not to scratch. She told me how she stayed on her best behaviour so she didn't attract the attention of the nuns because she saw what they did to the children who stepped out of line. But sometimes, if she was being treated too badly, she'd run off to find her mother who lived in the staff quarters and her mom would set those nuns straight!

My research expanded to include first-account testimonies from others who had survived residential schools, and I realized quickly that Kohkum had been exceptionally lucky to have her mother nearby since complete separation from family and identity was the first order of business for these institutions.

Perhaps you can take a moment to imagine a child that you love around the age of three or four. Now, imagine that child ripped from the arms of their mother by strangers in long black robes or an RCMP officer, and taken far from home. They are deposited in some institution where they don't speak the language and have no idea what's happening. They're stripped of their clothes, thrown in a cold shower, doused with lice remover, and given a school uniform. Then their hair is shorn in a fashion resembling a prisoner, which is more disturbing when you consider that in Indigenous culture, hair is a part of identity and is only cut for periods of mourning. Throughout these rough acts of degradation, your small child is subjected to a torrent of verbal abuse. They may not understand the words, but one in particular is repeated often — *savage*. It must be an important word. Finally, they are given a number. That number will be their identity going forward.

Over the years, their name, like their parents, begins to fade from memory. Time passes in a blur of fear, as your child fends off the attacks of the so-called men and women of God who abuse their body, their mind, and their spirit. Then, after they've lost their language, identity, and family — after being violated and degraded for years on end, they're thrown back out into the world. The white world. Broken. Alone.

This was just a taste of what life was like for countless survivors after residential school. Can you understand now the fallout of this legacy? Broken families, addictions, dysfunction, and all the elements that accompany trauma.

I resolved to work harder. To give voice to survivors and this generation. For their truth to reverberate into the minds and hearts of the world. I began the difficult task of trying to track down historical documents or policies concerned with residential schools and my horror only grew as I read how the government and church deliberately set out to "kill the Indian in the child." Countless calls for investigations were buried and ignored along with the reports of violence and murder taking place within those walls. These schools were an intentional tool of government-sanctioned Indigenous genocide that operated for decades right under everyone's noses.

Just like me, so many of the children or grandchildren of residential school survivors didn't even know about residential schools, or as they're more often called in the United States, boarding schools. Partly our lack of awareness was due to the shame and stigma that whipped these children into lifelong silence. But widespread ignorance was also by design. The national political, religious, and economic powers wanted society to be left in the dark. This made their colonialist agenda of land stealing, resource appropriation, and Indigenous "assimilation" (a.k.a. extermination) much easier to pull off.

My journey of reconnection to my Indigenous bloodlines and culture was not all horror and rage. Quite the opposite! I discovered that my kohkum belonged to the Michel First Nation. The Michel are descendants of a great leader named Chief Louis Kwarakwante (the Sun Traveller). He was born in the Iroquois village of Caughnawaga near Montreal on October 17, 1782. He was an expert fur trader, trapper, and hunter, and in his teen years he assisted as a voyageur guide for the North West Company. He travelled west to the mountains and settled in what is now Alberta. He married a Cree woman and a Sekanaise woman, fathering an alliance between these tribes along with a legacy of descendants. He was a leader, a dreamer, a traveller, and a reconciler. He is my great-great-great-great-grandfather.

Chief Kwarakwante died sometime between 1845 and 1856, but he is not forgotten. His ancestry is recognized as one of the oldest lineages of tribes in North America and his genetics are preserved at the Fifth International Congress of Blood Transfer of Hematology in Paris, France. It is believed that he is buried somewhere in the Rocky Mountains near Jasper, Alberta. It is a dream of mine to one day find his grave so I can pay my respects. Until I do, there is still much I can do to honour his legacy. Like getting his ancestral land (and mine) reinstated for starters.

Despite our renowned heritage — our blood and lineage preserved and protected in Paris, thank you very much — the Michel First Nation has no official land, or even status with the Canadian federal government. Their ancestral land had been protected on a reserve, located west of St. Albert, Alberta. Starting in the late 1930s an Indian agent representing the Canadian government convinced Michel members to assimilate in exchange for farming tools and training (which in many cases never came about) along with the promise that they would not have to send their children to residential schools. The Indian agent's agreement meant that he actually bought the land — for next to nothing — and promptly sold it to European settlers. The final blow against Michel First

Nation came in 1958 when the nation was involuntarily enfranchised and most members lost their Indian status and "assimilated" into the mainstream. The people's connection to the land and to each other in community was severed. The nation dissolved and its reserve lands were sold by the government of Canada.

The descendants of the Michel First Nation have been fighting for recognition and reinstatement of their rights for years in Canada's court systems. There is an elected Chief and council with upwards of a thousand members. Many have regained their Indian status. My kohkum regained hers before her death and her children and grandchildren, including me, are in the process of reinstatement. I'm doing this to honour her legacy and to stand in my sovereignty, not because I want to become a ward of the Indian Act.

My research into the Michel First Nation turned up another surprise. I learned that the house my dad bought, where my uncle and aunt now live, was the first settler home constructed on Michel First Nation's territory over one hundred years ago. My Michel Band relatives are buried on the lands surrounding the farm. This was the farm from my vision where I saw skeletons rising from the ground and dancing over the land. I did not know this history of the farm when I lived there.

Neither did my father when he purchased the land to make a home there with his Michel First Nation wife and children.

Suddenly I understood the meaning of that powerful yet perplexing vision. These were my displaced ancestors dancing out of their graves and calling me to unravel the truths of the injustice that had been done to them, along with the countless atrocities experienced by Indigenous Peoples in Canada and beyond. They called me from my own grave and infused me with their power and blessing so that I could rise up and take my rightful place in the generational work of our people. What an honour it was to understand the meaning of this sacred message, all these years later. What an honour to be part of this family.

The more I learned over the years, the more I fell in love with the strength of the Indigenous nations — the bonds we share, and ways we have managed to hold on to our culture and identity despite the horrors visited upon us by European settlers and their descendants. But my research was creating a new problem for me as well. The blood of those European settlers also ran through my veins. Oppressor and oppressed commingled in the chambers of my beating heart and I did not know how to reconcile the anger, heartbreak, disgust, and confusion of it all. I could not expel half of who I was, but I could not make peace with it either. Reconciliation at its most basic level felt impossible for me.

I carried this inner tension into my work as a journalist. I resolved to work harder, determined to give voice to my people, allowing their truth to reverberate in the minds and hearts of the world. It is my work to push through the silence, the gaslighting, and the denial with which our stories are met from mainstream culture.

In 2021, many Canadians expressed shock and recoiled with sadness when the unmarked graves of thousands of Indigenous children were found on the grounds of former residential schools. But survivors in Canada told the Truth and Reconciliation Commission about the murder of these children over six years ago. This wasn't new news. And not everyone was shocked and saddened. Those who deny the evidence, deny the Indigenous experience, still exist—even with the bones of our children right under their noses. There are others who simply don't care. Sometimes I want to scream in frustration when yet another white person shrugs off the legacy of residential schools as "ancient history," preferring instead to blame the suffering of Indigenous Peoples on their own so-called laziness, weakness, or morally inferior character.

But I don't scream. I remind myself that at one point, I didn't know the truth. I remind myself that the majority of people do respond with compassion and outrage when they understand the truth. So I buckle down and do the work I can do. I report. I write. And I push and push and push for Indigenous voices to be heard outside of our own circles. Because reconciliation will only ever be achieved when ignorance gives way to truth on a global scale.

IN THE SUMMER OF 2021, I had an opportunity to bring just one of the many stories connected to residential schools to the international stage. I drove to Carlisle, Pennsylvania, to join representatives from the Rosebud Sioux Tribe for a transfer ceremony and three-day cross-country journey. I was working for *National Geographic* to cover the historic repatriation of the skeletal remains of nine Lakota youth who died attending the Carlisle Indian Boarding School. The Rosebud Sioux Tribe had been actively advocating for over six years and at last it was happening.

Throughout the decades, Native American children had been forcibly taken from their families and distributed thousands of miles across the country in "re-education" schools, in order to learn the ways of the white man. In 1897, nine children between the ages of ten and nineteen died at Carlisle Indian Boarding School and their remains were buried in a cemetery on the former school grounds. Since that time, the Rosebud Sioux Tribe has kept their memories alive and never lost their determination to bring their children home. I was honoured to be a part of this historic moment, so many years in the making.

The repatriation event was led by the Sicangu Youth Council with support from elders and tribal leadership. The first night at the hotel in Pennsylvania, I met with the youth and the Lakota community members who would be escorting the remains of their relatives all the way home to South Dakota. It was an evening of tears as the young people expressed how challenging a journey this had already been, how heartbroken they were over the fate of their lost relatives, and how relieved they were to be bringing them home at last. It took everything in me not to bawl my eyes out.

Seeking to keep my own emotions at bay, I stepped outside for a breath. It was about 10:00 p.m. The summer sun was down and the moon was bright and comforting. I walked into a small field across from the hotel to take a moment to pray. Suddenly little pops of light were exploding around me. Gasping, I couldn't believe my eyes. Fireflies! I'd only ever seen them in movies and had dreamed of seeing them in person my whole life. They were breathtaking.

I stood in the field, surrounded by these small but brilliant bursts of light. *Pop, pop, pop.* There and gone. I thought of all the lost children whose light had been taken from them. I thought too of the missing and murdered Indigenous women and girls and the countless flames that had been extinguished before their time. All these beautiful beings of light, forever lost to this world. My tears ran freely.

Pop, pop, pop. The light kept coming, all around me and I felt hope rekindling. The Lakota youth in the building beside me were a living reminder that our light has not been extinguished. It will never be extinguished. As long as there is family. As long as there is love. As long as there are voices to call out to each other, our flame will continue to burn. I thanked God for sending me this sign. I felt Him with me. I turned towards the hotel, ready to return to the warmth inside.

For the next few days I journeyed with the Lakota youth, their chaperones, and the bones of their ancestors. They were long, taxing days — physically, emotionally, and spiritually — filled with ceremony, prayers, traditional songs, honourings and feasts in the various native communities where we stopped along the way. The welcome we received when we finally reached the Rosebud Sioux Tribe in South Dakota was stunning. Hundreds of Lakota lined the highway, some standing on vehicles, or riding horses, but most on foot. The numbers swelled as we drew closer to the reservation, crowding the streets, their fists of solidarity held high in the air.

The burial ceremony was an elaborate affair. Drums, singing, and tears accompanied the small pine boxes throughout their wake, funeral, and the moment when they were finally laid to rest in their territorial ground, back in the comforting womb of Mother Earth, where they belonged. Each was buried with a star blanket, handmade traditional clothing, traditional medicine, pemmican, sage, and gifts from family members. They were no longer the lost. They were home.

I would like to share one final story from my time with the Lakota people.

During my visit, I was given the opportunity to fulfill another one of my lifelong dreams — horseback riding on those beautiful wild lands. I visited a ranch that specialized in working with people who have endured trauma — survivors of violence, offenders, troubled youth — and paired them with formerly abused horses.

Greg Grey Cloud, our guide, and manager of the program, asked me if I wanted to do a traditional spirit-connecting ceremony with the horses. I must admit I was a bit nervous because I didn't know what it entailed. But something was pulling on my spirit, so I agreed. He led seven horses into the round paddock and then directed me to stand in the middle with him.

"You just need to wait here," Greg explained. "The horse will choose you. Trust the process."

A couple of ranch hands encouraged the horses into a gallop. They ran around the perimeter twice in one direction and then twice the other way. I followed them, turning my body in a circle as they thundered around me, their manes flowing, nostrils snorting, and hooves pounding the hard-packed earth. The force of their power vibrated through every cell in my body.

Then the horses stopped and the silence was equally deafening. I waited as I'd been instructed. After a couple of minutes, one of the horses broke from the group and approached me. His red-and-chestnut coat blazed in the sunlight. He had white socks that showed off his large hoofs. I swallowed and stood as still as I could. *Trust the process, trust the process, trust the process*, I chanted in my mind.

The horse stopped in front of me, lowering his head so his liquid brown eyes could meet mine, his ears pricked forward in curiosity. I smelled his hay-sweetened breath as he huffed a greeting.

"That's Socks," Greg said, approaching the two of us. "Former rodeo horse. He used to be tied up and abused something terrible by his former owner." Socks's ears flicked backwards at the sound of Greg's approach, but he kept his gaze on me. "Socks ... he usually chooses leaders," said Greg, stepping to Socks's side and stroking his black mane. "But they don't know they're leaders yet."

I felt something catch at my throat.

"That's the thing," Greg continued. "The horses always choose the rider who is most like them. Socks is powerful, but he doesn't always know it. That abuse went deep. But you know, when he gets outside the fences here and into the pasture, he realizes he's free. And he realizes he's boundless. That's a sight to see."

The tears broke like a dam. That was me all right. For so many years, held back by the invisible restraints of former abuse. But I am a leader. I am coming into my own. I need only to step out of those enclosures built by fear. And then I will be truly free to live into the strength and power that I already possess.

I touched Socks on his whiskery velvet nose and thanked him for his gift.

"Ready to ride?" Greg asked.

- 12 -

DEMAND FOR MY WORK continued to grow, as did my hunger to keep covering the stories connected to Indigenous calls for justice within my own country. Naturally, the extraction industry loomed large in my coverage. The government-sanctioned actions of the oil and gas industry taking place illegally on Indigenous territory are one of the prime examples of the ongoing betrayal of and aggression against Canada's Indigenous population. Sovereign lands are trespassed on and decimated, peaceful land defenders are terrorized, beaten, and arrested by RCMP (who are also trespassing), not to mention the direct connection of the extraction industry to our missing and murdered women and girls—the list of human rights violations connected to the extraction industry is extensive. I'd been pitching an international series on this topic to the major media outlets for a while, but they weren't biting. But I wasn't giving up.

I was driven by the memory of one of my trips for the *National Observer* in the summer of 2020. While visiting the Wet'suwet'en First Nation Traditional Territories in so-called British Columbia with Wet'suwet'en Hereditary Chief Gisday'wa along with his wife and sister, we followed the industry roads up into the mountains and deep into pristine forest where Costal GasLink (CGL) had recently set up operation along the intended route for the forty-billion-dollar liquefied-natural-gas pipe they were constructing.

It was the first time Gisday'wa and his family had seen their land since CGL moved in. They were shocked and horrified at the sheer expanse of the environmental destruction wrought by the massive machines that lumbered over the land, leaving nothing recognizable in their wake. These were his hunting grounds, gutted and ruined. Trees had been ripped from their roots and yawning chasms like huge open graves scarred the land. Planted alongside this ruin was CGL's massive camp — rows and rows of utility trailers housing hundreds of workers. My skin crawled at the sight. These remote work camps, packed with men, are notorious for their demand for vulnerable Indigenous women and girls, many of whom are never seen again.

Gisday'wa, outraged and distraught, had choice words for the security worker who confronted him. "Why are you doing this to my lands? And why are you bringing all these men here to rape our women? Just like you people brought in the priests and the nuns to rape our children! You're doing this all over! You sons of bitches," he shouted, while his wife and sister sobbed behind him. The CGL employee looked bored, although he took a step back.

We left the camp and headed to a nearby RCMP post. Gisday'wa questioned two officers about why they were still there when the RCMP had agreed to pull out of Wet'suwet'en territories months before. He got no answers except that they were "working on" getting their patrol troops out. They had the same look of boredom in their eyes.

IT HAD BEEN SIX months since that trip with Chief Gisday'wa when in December 2020 I got the news that Al Jazeera English was interesting in backing my pitch to do an extensive feature series on the connections between the extraction industry and MMIWG. It was a big project and would require a lot of time and research, not to mention thousands of dollars. I was approved for a six-part written series and would work with photo-journalist Amber Bracken, a talented professional who has become a dear friend and who reports extensively on Indigenous communities. I flew into action, writing each chapter outline and submitting the proposal within days.

By February, I was heading back to Wet'suwet'en and Gitxsan territories, only this time I had backup. Amber was with me and Al Jazeera had my back. This made the work marginally less dangerous, but we weren't idiots. Multi-billion-dollar industries aren't exactly known for welcoming investigative reporters. If anything, they're known for playing dirty and the local RCMP didn't have a much better reputation. We knew we needed to be careful.

The first day we headed up to a secluded camp called Unist'ot'en, set up and occupied by Wet'suwet'en matri-arch Freda Huson. She'd set up her riverside camp at the sacred river of her ancestors called Wedzin Kwa — on her traditional land — directly in the path of the CGL pipeline and had been living there for over a decade. The rivers in Freda's territories are some of the last of their kinds in the world. They're clear and crisp and you can drink out of them without getting sick. Medicines, huckleberries, and traditional foods grow in abundance but they're now under threat. Indigenous and non-Indigenous supporters have joined Freda at her camp, also putting their lives on the line in order to protect the territory. It's a battle between industry, the governments who green-lit the project despite its illegality, and the police who enforce industry injunctions to bulldoze the pipeline through despite the fact that over twenty years ago, the Wet'suwet'en and Gitxsan Nations established their unceded Aboriginal title to this land in the Supreme Court of Canada. Their rights to their territory are unequivocal.

In early 2020, police raided the Unist'ot'en and other camps blocking the way of the pipeline. The world finally witnessed what had been going on for years when they saw social media footage of the violent arrests of peaceful Indigenous protesters defending their own land. This triggered massive protests across Canada that shut down railways, highways, and other major infrastructure for weeks, demanding that government and industry back down on the pipeline in Wet'suwet'en territory. A closed-door emergency meeting was held with Wet'suwet'en Hereditary Chiefs, the Minister of Crown-Indigenous Relations, and provincial representatives. The big meeting helped quell the protests but no real solution for the current dispute was reached. Everyone signed a Memorandum of Understanding to deal with implementing the title and rights on future projects. An MOU is an agreement between two or more parties, usually outlining action to resolve something. In this case, it was an agreement between the Hereditary Chiefs, the province, and the federal government. When the media attention settled down, work on the pipeline started back up.

At the time of our visit, Freda and her supporters were still living on the mountain and tensions were high, but police weren't actively arresting people. We had a good, daylong meeting with Freda. As we started to make our way back down the mountain, Amber wanted to stop and photograph some of the red dresses that hung alongside the road. The dresses—symbols of the missing and murdered Indigenous women and girls—were all over the place since this area is adjacent to the infamous Highway of Tears, where dozens of mostly Indigenous women have disappeared or have been found dead. I pulled the car over the best I could, parking against the high snowbanks on the side of the road. The ghostly dresses fluttered in the freezing wind. It was a hauntingly stark and beautiful sight. Amber wanted to walk back across a long, single-lane bridge that we had just crossed to grab some shots. I quickly lost sight of her in my rear-view mirror.

Suddenly a white CGL industry truck drove slowly by our car. The window was down and the driver was recording me with a hand-held camera. Odd, but not that odd. CGL was known for surveillance activities near their job sites. Then an identical white truck slowly cruised past, only this one was not marked with the CGL logo and RCMP officers were driving. They too lowered their window as they passed. Both officers stared at me as if I were a menace. A thin film of sweat instantly broke out on my forehead.

I shared the encounter with Amber when she returned.

"Yeah, the cops drive around here with industry looking for protesters," she said.

Hmmm, that's an interesting partnership, I thought, but said nothing.

I pulled back onto the road and started to make my way down the mountain. A few metres ahead, both white trucks were waiting for me. One of the RCMP officers motioned for me to pull over. Now this was starting to get weird. We were in the middle of nowhere, hadn't done anything wrong, and he wanted us to pull over?

We stopped. The CGL truck immediately pulled out, drove a full circle around our SUV, the driver still recording us with his video camera, before gunning his truck and roaring off in a cloud of exhaust. The RCMP made no move to stop them.

The officer approached the car. His body language was tense and confrontational. I checked my cell phone. No signal. I got nervous. He told us to step out of the car. I got even more nervous. "What are you doing up here?" the officer asked once we had joined him on the road. Amber was recording with her camera and I started recording on my cell phone for backup. I always record interactions with police. It's just good practice as a journalist—in my many encounters with them, I'd come to know police to lie. Amber had reminded me I didn't have to tell them anything, but I felt anxious and just wanted to follow the rules and keep it civil.

"We're journalists. We just came from Unist'ot'en camp. We're doing a story for Al Jazeera English," I said.

"Al Ja—what?"

"It's an international media company."

"Uh-huh. Can I see your licence?"

As I handed it over, Amber spoke up. "Why did you stop us? What did we do?"

"Well, it's just standard for us to stop anyone up

here," the officer replied. Amber rolled her eyes. She's blond, white, confident, and well-versed in dealing with the cops. She wasn't having it. But I—brown, Indigenous, nervous, with my own very different history with cops—well, I was freaked out.

It felt like he was fishing to find a reason to keep us there, but after a few more questions he eventually told us we could go. Amber called out questions to him as he sauntered back to his vehicle, but he ignored her and slammed the truck door in her face.

The drive off the mountain was forty-five minutes long. The roads were winding and slippery with snow. My heart was racing after that encounter and I had to take several deep breaths and remind myself to concentrate on my driving. About ten minutes later I noticed the big white truck was behind me. I tried to ignore them. They got closer. I gripped the steering wheel tighter. A red dress hanging on a tree danced in the wind as we drove by.

"Amber, I think the cops are following us," I said in a tight voice.

She looked back. Yes, it was them all right. I felt my tires slip a bit on the steep snowing road and eased off the accelerator. No matter my speed, if I sped up or slowed down, they matched it, keeping their distance the way a wolf follows the caribou it has chosen.

"Oh God, Amber, I just want to get off this mountain," I said as my breathing got faster. I felt so frightened that I started crying. *Get it together, Brandi!*

"It's going to be okay. They're just intimidating us." Amber tried to assure me.

It seemed to take forever but we finally reached the bottom of the mountain and I could catch my breath. They roared past us and disappeared from view.

That night at the hotel I had my first panic attack in years. It was so severe that I thought I was having a heart attack. Thank God I was sharing a room with Amber. I woke her up, convinced I was dying, but she knew exactly what was going on for me — as she always does.

"Okay, Brandi." Her voice was gentle and grounding. "We're going to breathe together. And we can pray too, even though I haven't prayed in a while. Ready . . . ?"

I eventually fell asleep listening to a prayer meditation that Amber found on her phone.

I managed to pull through for the rest of the assignment but felt uneasy on the drive back home. So few people understand the weight of the stories and the emotional toll of this work. I knew that no amount of experience, healing, or recognition could shield me from it. Covering stories of murder, pain, corruption, and the threat that comes with it—I feel it. I always feel it. I've also told myself that this is what makes me a good storyteller. And while that's true, there are limits. Should telling the truth cost me my life?

The threats to my well-being are psychological *and* physical. Where the tsunami of government and industry interests smashes against Indigenous Peoples who are standing up for their rights—with blockages, protests, encampments—it is dangerous.

In July 2020, I was back in British Columbia, this time for the *National Observer*, to cover the rising tensions between the non-native townspeople in Blue River, British Columbia, and a group of Indigenous land defenders known as the Tiny House Warriors. The Warriors were blocking the Trans Mountain Pipeline (formerly known as the Kinder Morgan Pipeline) expansion from cutting a path of destruction through their traditional territory. Settler residents were angry. They wanted the pipeline and the work that went with it, and they were sick of the Indians across the highway who were holding up progress. No, it did not matter that the pipeline violated the sovereignty and land rights of the Secwepemc people. The settlers decided to stage a protest of their own and I hustled from my hotel room to live-stream the event.

This was during the Black Lives Matter worldwide protests and only a month and a half since George Floyd was murdered by police officer Derek Chauvin in Minneapolis. Racial tensions were high, as was the potential for violence to break out on this assignment. I'd spoken to the Tiny House Warriors, who told me how they were regularly harassed and surveilled by police. The police even placed snipers in the bushes during heated escalations. The threats against these land defenders were real.

The cops were present for the settler protest as well although they were in plain clothes, almost as if to minimize their show of force against the protesting townspeople — "We're here but we're casual. We're with you." Some choice words were yelled from a couple of the settlers to the Indigenous land defenders, but no physical violence ensued. After returning to the hotel, Neskonlith Chief Judy Wilson, who is Secwepemc and a passionate land defender, invited me to go for a drive with her and her eighty-year-old mother, Minnie. We drove for two hours through winding mountain highways while Chief Judy shared some of her experiences as an Indigenous leader attempting to protect her land against government and industry's economic interests. She gets bullied and threatened, lied to repeatedly, and treated with absolute disdain. A couple of years prior, she travelled to Houston, Texas, to present her people's concerns to the executives of the Trans Mountain Pipeline and to make it clear that consent was not granted for expanding the project into Indigenous lands.

"The Kinder Morgan CEO was so furious with me that he stormed out of the room while I was talking." Judy shook her head. "But that's Texas for you. And that's where all the oil is connected to."

When we got back from our drive—and back into cell range—I saw an odd notification on my phone: IHIT now followed me on Periscope. Periscope was the online streaming app I had used to live-stream the protest earlier in the day. The IHIT account was verified so I was naturally curious about it. When I clicked on the profile, chills ran up my spine. It was the Integrated Homicide Investigation Team out of Burnaby, BC— the largest homicide unit in Canada, responsible for investigating homicides, suspicious deaths, and missing persons where foul play is suspected.

I could see that they had viewed my coverage of events that day. Why the hell were they following my account? I was in the middle of nowhere and had little promotion of my reporting that day. They wouldn't have come across my coverage by accident. Now I was really curious. Who else were they following? Chills again when I realized they were only following twelve accounts. One of them was a police account and I clicked on it. The Houston Texas Sheriff's Office. Chief Judy's conversation with me immediately sprang to mind. Whatever the connection between the Texas police, this homicide unit, and me — an Indigenous woman covering the pipeline protests — it certainly felt like I was lining up as a potential target.

But just to be sure I wasn't spinning stories in my mind, I called my editor at the *National Observer*, Laurie Few — another incredible powerhouse in this business — to run the situation by her.

Laurie, a clear-headed lawyer, was immediately on high alert. "I want you to let others in the hotel know about it and then I want you to barricade your door for the night. Tomorrow I want you to go home." She was brooking no argument from me. I was supposed to spend another couple of days on assignment there but it wasn't worth the risk.

I was scared shitless that night. I locked the window and shut the curtains. I had Elaysia with me. She was two, and I often brought her with me when I travelled as I didn't like to spend too much time away from her. Travis had also joined me to help take care of her. I certainly regretted my decision to bring her along that night, let me tell you. I pulled her crib away from the windows, snuggled it close to my bed, and tried not to imagine a brick coming through my window or bad guys waiting outside my door to ambush me.

This wasn't just paranoia. There was a lot of money at stake and many powerful people who did not want this story out. The pipeline is now owned by the Canadian government. Prime Minister Justin Trudeau bought it in 2018 after Kinder Morgan pulled the plug due to uncertainty. This state-owned multi-billion-dollar pipeline has a lot of powerful stakeholders. Although Justin Trudeau has claimed that his number one priority is reconciliation with Indigenous Peoples in Canada, his actions have proved otherwise when it comes to upholding Indigenous rights. He has demonstrated time and time again that he advances reconciliation only on his terms — and only when it suits him. He still allows Indigenous Peoples to be forcibly removed from their lands such as was the case with the Trans Mountain development and the Wet'suwet'en crisis. He even brought in army troops to raid the Unist'ot'en Wet'suwet'en camp more than once to violently remove Indigenous opposition.

To Justin Trudeau, I say this: Respecting Indigenous rights has to happen on all fronts, not just when it makes a good photo opportunity or helps to get votes.

THAT NIGHT IN THE hotel I tossed and turned. When morning finally came, I couldn't check out quickly enough. While Travis and I were packing up the car, a movement across the street caught my eye.

The day before, Indigenous elders had held a ceremony there to remember our MMIWG and the bushes were festooned with red dresses. Now these dresses were shaking furiously and I thought it might be the young bear that was rumoured to be running around town. But I saw the outline of a man and realized he was tearing the red dresses down.

"Oh, my God, he's ripping down the dresses!" I told Travis, thrusting Elaysia's stroller into his hands. "Can you keep your eye on her? I need to go over there."

"Yes, but be careful," he said.

I started recording on my cell phone and raced across the road. He had just ripped the last dress down and was storming out of the bush.

"Hey! What are you doing?" I demanded.

No answer. He was just a middle-aged white guy with

a baseball cap striding towards me, his face red with anger. He saw me recording and turned suddenly, walking towards the highway.

"What are you doing that for? Why did you rip the dresses down?" I persisted.

"Because they're trash and they belong in the garbage," he shouted back at me.

"Trash?" I felt that familiar heat blooming in the pit of my stomach at his words. "Do you realize what those represent?"

"Oh, fuck off," he spat, and walked off.

I turned to look at the desecrated dresses. Their vibrant red fabric crumpled and soiled, some bearing muddy boot prints where the man had ground them into the muck.

Just more trash to be tossed and forgotten.

When would our Indigenous women and girls be more than this?

I knew the stats. In Canada, Indigenous women and girls make up just 4 per cent of the population, yet account for 24 per cent of female homicide victims. The vast majority of MMIWG have been in the foster care system. Indigenous women are twelve times more likely to be missing or murdered than any other woman in Canada. When compared only to Caucasian women, the number jumps to Indigenous women being sixteen times more likely to be missing or murdered.

And why not? Predators seek out Indigenous women because they understand we are vulnerable. When we go missing or turn up dead, the police are less likely to investigate, and our justice systems don't prosecute or convict these perpetrators. The mainstream media hardly covers us in the news either, probably due to the rampant indifference and disdain within mainstream culture towards Indigenous Peoples. I've heard our missing and murdered women and girls described as "just another dead Indian," or "just a runaway," or "out on a drunk."

A body in the Red River, a bloody condom, a crushed dress — trash, trash, trash.

The heat in my core burst into flame.

I am not trash.

I've covered countless stories of mothers, daughters, sisters, friends who have been lost to this epidemic of violence. I've stood at the places where their bodies were dumped. I've held their loved ones as they mourn. I've shared the pain of their injustice.

We are not trash.

In a country like Canada, admired around the world as a bastion of human rights, I often wonder how they've been able to get away with this for so long. Well, time's up. I was sick of collecting the stories off dead bodies. I was sick of being treated like I was someone they could threaten and intimidate. They didn't know who they were dealing with. I wasn't the hunted, I was the hunter, and it was time to hunt down and stop the violence driven by political, economic, institutional, and societal racism.

I looked across the street at my little daughter, sucking her fist in her stroller. I clenched my own fists and headed back to her, already composing the feature story in my mind. I still burned inside, but now I burned for justice. I burned for those whose bodies had been left cold. My words were fire and I was ready to set the world ablaze.

- 13 -

I'VE ALWAYS BEEN INSPIRED by the annual phenomenon of salmon returning to their spawning grounds. Their instinct and drive to return to the place where they were born is legendary. Their goal is singular and simple — get home. And they will do whatever it takes to achieve it.

Some groups of salmon swim over three thousand kilometres in from the Pacific Ocean and up into the freshwater rivers of British Columbia to return to their place of birth. Their path is treacherous. They face predator after predator, starting with the killer whales and seals that wait to ambush them in the ocean channels. Eagles are a constant danger from the sky, scooping up salmon with razor-sharp talons. The bears and wolves line up along the riverways to hunt and have their fill as well. Environmental obstacles are as daunting as the gauntlet of predators. Salmon swim against the current, the opposite way of the natural river flow! They face rapids and waterfalls. Salmon can jump up to two metres — that's about as high as an Olympic athlete can jump — but that doesn't mean some of them don't die of exhaustion when water levels are high and the water flow is particularly strong. And during years when the water levels are low, many salmon die when they become beached in the shallows.

It's hard to imagine how even one salmon makes it home, but they do. And every time I feel myself flagging on my path, I think of these miracles of nature. We are all marked for greatness, but we have a choice. Give up or keep going. It doesn't matter what you've been through, how much money you have, where you're from, as long as you believe and never give up, you will get through. Believe me, I did.

THESE DAYS I CAN barely handle all the requests from editors, organizations, and people asking me to write or speak at their events. I've dreamed of these days for a long time, and then worked my butt off to get here. I'm finally in a position where I can call the shots and pitch the stories I want to tell, no longer begging for our stories to be heard. It's happening!

Elaysia is four now and she's grown up partially on the road with me. I like having her around. It's different being a mom when you're older. It's also different being a mom when you're not stressed out and in survival mode. I'm able to enjoy all the little things. Yes, I've felt guilty for not having given my older children the best of me because I had them when I was young and vulnerable. But I've learned to forgive myself and have asked their forgiveness for my shortcomings. We are all pretty close now.

Faith is in university to become a teacher, Luke is going into dentistry, and Dani is finishing her last year of high school. She tells me she wants to travel North America on a baby-blue moped after high school. She's my free spirit. I tell her and all my children to chase their heart callings. I will love and support them in whatever they do. We've always been together getting through this life and we'll always have our special bond that way.

My kids have witnessed how hard I've worked. They've watched my career rise and fall. They watched me get back up after every blow to the ground. They know that I easily could have ended up a drunk, an addict, homeless, or depressed lying in a bed on welfare. But I clawed my way out. Dream by dream. Prayer by prayer. Determined that my own children would be less encumbered, as they climbed the ladder of life, than the generations who came before.

That is not to say I'm finished with healing. I used to think that one day I would "arrive" and have it all together in my life. But I've learned that healing is an ongoing journey. We are never really "there" until we leave this earthly realm. And that's okay, because I love this beautiful journey of discovery, of inspiration and provocations. I'm still working on things, but I've come a hell of a long way. I'm filled with the relief that comes from forgiveness. I was confronted with the task of choosing to forgive the men who stole my innocence. It wasn't an option for me not to. Because I believe holding unforgiveness would be like allowing them to hold me captive forever. It would grow like a poison and choke my light and power rendering me unable to achieve anything meaningful. I forgive them. I've released them from that inner chamber of trauma and into the hands of the One who is the ultimate judge. Sometimes I've had to do it over and over, forgive those monsters. It took me over twenty years to speak about what happened to me. Now I'm filled with relief and peace that I don't have to carry them or their actions with me anymore.

I've also come a long way in facing my fears. I'm

writing this chapter from my nineteenth-floor room at the ritzy Pan Pacific hotel in Vancouver. To my right, I see the stunning skyline of downtown set against the backdrop of snow-capped mountains kissed by the orange and pink light of the rising sun. To my left, I see the Pacific Ocean that, from this height, looks to stretch out into infinity. And that's how big my future feels right now.

I'm here celebrating one of the greatest victories of my life so far. Yesterday, I finally faced my long-standing and seemingly unshakable phobia of flying. I hadn't been on a plane since my previous attempt to face down this fear that resulted in months of lockdown in the psych ward. And while I knew that it wasn't the flying that actually landed me there, the phobia had attached itself to that moment and grown ten times in size. For over ten years, I've been driving to my assignments — sometimes as far as California — rather than flying, and I'd turned down a number of opportunities that required flying. Enough was enough.

After a couple of failed attempts to board a plane, one instance of literally banging on the closed door of the plane as it began its taxi, hundreds of prayers, and plenty of emotional support, here I am in Vancouver. Yesterday, I flew here!

I booked round-trip tickets for a day and one night for the express purpose of kicking this fear in the butt. My sweet, patient, wise, amazing therapist Mary-Anne agreed to come with me. I felt all the familiar terror during boarding and takeoff, and clasped Mary-Anne's hand tight as I squeezed my eyes shut in prayer. Honestly, I expected it to be just like before — I'd make it through the agony of the flight and landing, and slowly over time it might be less horrible.

But somewhere up there above the clouds, something miraculous occurred. I don't know how else to explain it except to say that God showed up for me. I knew this was the moment for me: it was time to let go and trust the process. And just like that, suddenly I was free. It was so glorious. That feeling. That knowing. Looking down on the majesty of the clouds, the skyline, the hustle and bustle of our little lives so small below, I realized it was over. The fear had broken.

I knew in that instant that my life had changed. It wasn't just about a plane and being scared to fly. This was about breaking through other boundaries and overcoming challenges in all the areas of my life where I felt stuck. I've always said that if I could get over the fear of flying, I could get over anything in my life! Here I am. Free to walk through the doors that are opening for me. I'm free to travel and go to the ends of the earth to bring our stories to the forefront. The sky is no longer the limit. From this view, my future looks as boundless as the ocean.

That's how I view our people too. We've been through a hell of a journey, but we are still here. Despite the tools of colonialism that have been operating for centuries and continue today via the Indian Act, inequality, enforced poverty, and the breaking of sovereign Treaties. Canada has freeloaded off the resources on Indigenous territories such gold, oil, gas, timber, water, and land while the First Peoples are left with crumbs. Yet we have endured.

Despite the stealing, abusing, and killing of Indigenous children via the evil legacy of the Sixties Scoop, residential school systems, and the underfunding of schools on reserves. Our family structures have been smashed, our identities stripped away, many of us are broken and cannot find that spark of hope, our youth are committing suicide — But. We. Persist.

We are healing. And we are rising.

Metis revolutionary leader Louis Riel prophesied in 1885: "My people will sleep for one hundred years, but when they awake, it will be the artists who give them their spirit back."

We have awoken. We are reclaiming our voices of fire.

There are 634 recognized First Nations in Canada, which represent more than 50 nations and 50 Indigenous languages. According to the 2016 Canada Census, there are 1.67 million Metis, Inuit, and First Nations people in Canada, making up 4.9 per cent of the population. But we are the fastest growing population! Our numbers increased by 42.5 per cent between 2006 and 2016. Which means we are also the youngest population.

This is the Generation of Fire and we are rising to take our place in this troubled world. We are journalists, doctors, lawyers, CEOs, dentists, artists, and teachers. We are the caretakers of the sacred lands, the waters, and the medicines given to us by our Creator. We are the walking prayers of our ancestors. Our blood memory holds their wisdom and we call on them to help solve the current environmental, political, and economic crises that threaten the existence of all. We rise to take our rightful place, leading the way to a better world.

We lead, but we do not do this alone. We are not the only ones in need of healing. Our wounded world cries out for it. Our society calls out for it. If we do not heal the growing divisions between people, we will all be ripped asunder along with our wounded planet.

Reconciliation isn't going to happen easily; however, it's happening now more than ever. I've been a journalist for over ten years and I've witnessed the shifting landscape of reconciliation in Canada. More allies from all walks of life are showing up to support Indigenous rights, to mourn at the graves of the children who died at residential schools, and to hear from us about the history of the wrongs committed against the Indigenous nations. This matters. It is far from enough, but it is a start. We have a long journey ahead and we must equip ourselves with the compass of truth to guide us along the way.

THERE IS AN ANCIENT Anishinaabe prophecy about the time of the Seventh Fire:

> It is this time that the light-skinned race will be given a choice between two roads. One road will be green and lush, and very inviting. The other road will be black and charred, and walking it will cut their feet. In the prophecy, the people decide to take neither road, but instead turn back, to remember and reclaim the wisdom of those who came before them. If they choose the right road, then the Seventh Fire will light the Eighth and final fire — an eternal fire of peace,

love, brotherhood, and sisterhood. If the light-skinned race makes the wrong choice of the roads, then the destruction which they brought with them in coming to this country will come back at them and cause much suffering and death to all Earth's people.

This prophecy reminds us that all races have a part to play in determining our future fate, and learning to reconcile our differences may be among the most urgent work of our time. Those who will lead the way are those of us who have already learned the work of reconciliation from the inside out.

I am mixed blood, carrying the light-skinned bloodlines of my father. I am direct descendant of the Sun Traveller. I carry the bloodlines of the Iroquois and Cree nations through my mother. I carry within me the bloodlines of reconciliation.

I know my work in the world and I'm not stopping anytime soon. I pray the words that I write and the stories I tell, including my own, will move souls with inspiration to rise and take their place to walk the road of purpose Creator has for them. I add my voice to those who cry out for justice—the living and the lost.

We will be heard, we will be seen, and we will kindle the fires of justice across these lands. And we will not stop until the world is ablaze with hope, with peace, and with love.

I am Brandi Morin.

I'm a proud Cree/Iroquois/Frenchwoman from the lands of my ancestors in Treaty 6 Territories of the Michel First Nation.

I am granddaughter. I am daughter. I am sister. I am mother. I am survivor. I am warrior. I am a voice of fire.

Help is available for those who have experienced
sexual violence.

For immediate emotional assistance in Canada,
contact the national, independent, toll-free 24/7
crisis call line at 1-844-413-6649. This service
is offered through the Inquiry on Missing
and Murdered Indigenous Women and Girls.
Services are available in English, French, Cree,
Anishnaabemowin (Ojibway) and Inuktitut.

More support is available from the Canadian
Association of Sexual Assault Centres at
604-876-2622 and info@casac.ca or Kids Help Phone
at 1-800-668-6868 and www.kidshelpphone.ca.

In the United States, contact the RAINN Crisis
Support Line at 800-656-HOPE (4673) and
www.rainn.org to speak with a counsellor. This
national sexual assault hotline partners with more
than one thousand local sexual assault service
providers across the country.

More support is available from the Coalition to Stop
Violence Against Native Women at 505-243-9199
and www.csvanw.org.

– ACKNOWLEDGEMENTS –

TO KARYN PUGLIESE FOR encouraging me to write my story; to TransAtlantic Agency — Samantha Haywood and Laura Cameron — for sensing the spark in my vision and guiding me to write this book; to House of Anansi Press — Michelle MacAleese, Semareh Al-Hillal, Karen Brochu, Jessey Glibbery, Alysia Shewchuk, Lucia Kim, Chandra Wohleber, Tilman Lewis, Debby de Groot, Laura Chapnick, Zoe Kelsey, and Ricky Lima — for taking the chance on me and fully believing in this work; to Joanna Henry whose hard work and edits helped bring this book to life with colour and beauty; to Sharifah Marsden for allowing us to use her artwork on the cover; to Carla Bower at Al Jazeera English who helped me become a great writer; to my former editor Laurie Few for her straight talk and for modelling power and grace;

to the *Toronto Star*'s op-ed editor Scott Colby for always supporting my work; to APTN *National News* for hiring/investing in me; to Reverend Peter Dyck who counselled me as a child and always told me God had a big purpose for my life; to Pastors Carmen and Steve Lynne for always encouraging me to reach for the dreams of my heart and lifting me and my kids up in prayer; to Carson Mills who gave me the opportunity of a lifetime at the *Rep/Ex*; to Deborah, the very first editor who took me under her wing at the *Red River Valley Echo* all those years ago; to Mary-Anne for your revolutionary ministry of counselling and support; to Maxine for all your love through all these years; to Leslie for your unwavering example of faith and friendship; to Lee, my longest sustained friend for the adventurous journey we've shared on this wild ride of life; to Pastor Archie Binnie for being like a second father and upholding me in guidance and prayer; to Milt and Yvonne Owen for your steady assurance, love, encouragement, and patience with me; to Uncle Paul and family who I can always phone for any reason at all—you lift me up; to Travis for being a good father to Elaysia; to my siblings and our extended family—I hope this book helps us all heal, reconcile, and reconnect to our powerful roots; and to all my friends who've shown me love and support. I'm just getting started. Hiy hiy.

– NOTE ON ARTWORK –

THE ARTWORK ON THE cover of *Our Voice of Fire* is a painting entitled "Her Solo" by Sharifah Marsden, an Anishinaabekwe (Ojibwe woman).

The painting represents a woman singing her new song. Before she receives a new song, she provides a tobacco offering and prayer. Then the ceremony begins, which takes place in quiet, still, and peaceful solitude. In taking the time to sit in solitude, she renews her capacity to hear, see, feel, and receive what the Creator sends to her. When the woman has completed her seeking and sensing, she receives her song. With this song comes a drumbeat rhythm, words, and instructions for the song's purpose, whether it be for healing, war, or celebration. This image represents the first time she is singing the song, a solo, that has been gifted to her by the Creator.

Sharifah Marsden draws on her Anishinaabe roots and knowledge of Woodlands art to create unique works of diverse arts. These include painting at large and small scales, jewellery, and beadwork. She is known for her bentwood box titled "To Honour Our Indigenous Veterans," held in a collection at The Vancouver Museum. She is a graduate of Vancouver's Northwest Coast Jewellery Arts program, under established artist Haida/Kwakwaka'wakw artist Dan Wallace. Marsden has also worked with artists Richard Tetrault and Jerry Whitehead, among others, to complete Western Canada's largest mural, on the exterior of the Orwell Hotel in Vancouver. She presently lives in the interior of British Columbia with her family, where she continues to practise and teach.

BRANDI MORIN is an award-winning French/Cree/Iroquois journalist from Treaty 6, Alberta, Canada. For the last ten years Brandi has specialized in sharing Indigenous stories, which have influenced reconciliation in Canada's political, cultural, and social environments. She is one of Canada's most prominent voices on Indigenous issues. Morin has published or broadcast with the *New York Times*, *National Geographic*, the *Guardian*, the *Toronto Star*, Al Jazeera English, *Vice*, *Elle Canada*, CBC's *Power & Politics*, and the Aboriginal Peoples Television Network *National News*, among many other outlets. She won a Human Rights Reporting award from the Canadian Association of Journalists for her work with the CBC's Beyond 94 project tracking the progress of the Truth and Reconciliation Commission's Calls to Action. She has worked with Journalists for Human Rights, has presented to various university campuses in Canada and the United States regarding her work as an Indigenous journalist, and is in high demand for commentary and expertise on Indigenous topics.